DEDICATION

This book is dedicated with affection to Soccer "Nuts" of all ages and both sexes. We'll raise some questions, and try to give some answers to the training and playing situations of this relatively new game of Indoor Soccer.

Some parts of the book will apply to all players; some to beginners; some to intermediates; and some to experienced, accomplished players. By examining the game from different angles, we can uncover some of its secrets; improve our performance; and enjoy playing it more.

So let's have a go at it. May our touch on the ball be as smooth as silk and as soft as velvet, may our shots fly strong and true; may we be protected from injury; and may our sporting careers be long and happy.

ACKNOWLEDGEMENTS

I want to thank John Best, Claudia Best, Brian Flajole, and the staff of the Tacoma Stars of the Major Indoor Soccer League (MISL) for their help in providing access to the arena, locker rooms, and press box of their home floor, the Tacoma Dome, Tacoma, Washington. Special thanks to John Best for his review of parts of the manuscript.

No coverage of Indoor Soccer would be complete without input from the professional game. I am deeply grateful to the following coaches and players in the MISL for giving so freely of their views and opinions about the indoor game. As in all professional sports, there is movement of players and coaches from time to time from one team to another. The team affiliations given here are as of the time of our interview.

John Best, President of the Tacoma Stars
Tiemo Liekoski, Head Coach of the Cleveland Force
Peter Ward, Forward, Cleveland Force
Chris Vaccaro, Goal Keeper, Cleveland Force
Bernie James, Defender, Cleveland Force
Preki, Forward, Tacoma Stars
Mike Dowler, Goal Keeper, Tacoma Stars
Bob McNab, Head Coach of the Tacoma Stars
Keith Furphy, Forward, Kansas City Comets
Willy Roy, Head Coach of the Chicago Sting
Karl-Heinz Granitza, Forward, Chicago Sting
Hubert Birkenmeier, Goal Keeper, Chicago Sting
Neill Roberts, Defender, Chicago Sting
Keld Bordinggard, Forward, Wichita Wings
Steve Mclean, Defender, Wichita Wings
Roy Turner, Head Coach, Wichita Wings
Rick Benben, Head Coach, Kansas City Comets
Brian Quinn, Midfielder, San Diego Sockers
Jean Willrich, Midfielder, San Diego Sockers
Ron Newman, Head Coach, San Diego Sockers
Ken Cooper, Head Coach of the Baltimore Blast
Mark Kerlin, Forward, Baltimore Blast
Tim Wittman, Defender, Baltimore Blast
Stan Stamencovic, Forward, Baltimore Blast
Michael Collins, Midfielder, Baltimore Blast
Gordon Jago, Head Coach of the Dallas Sidekicks
Doc Lawson, Defender, Dallas Side Kicks
Louie Nanchoff, Forward, Dallas Sidekicks
Tatu, Forward, Dallas Sidekicks
Greg Blasingame, Defender, Tacoma Stars
Gary Heale, Forward, Tacoma Stars
Mark Peterson, Forward, Tacoma Stars

All illustrations are by: Manuel A. Ybarra III

Copyright© 1987 by Wes Leight

All rights reserved including the right of reproduction in any **form, except for brief** passages used in reviews.

Published by: Green Forest Products, 3012 143rd Ave. S.E. Snohomish, Washington, 98290

Manufactured in the U.S.A.

ORDERING COPIES

To order further copies of INDOOR SOCCER TACTICS AND **SKILLS, please** contact your bookstore or the publisher:

Green Forest Products
3012 143rd Ave. S.E.
Snohomish, WA 98290

(206) 334-7766

CONTENTS

Warm-Up 3
Equipment 7
ATTACKING PLAY 8
    Passing 8
    Using the diagrams 14
    Open and closed triangles 24
    Dribbling 26
    Change of pace 27
    The one-two 27
    Creating two on one 31
    The back-heel pass 33
    Using the boards 34
    The target man 39
    Shielding the ball 44
    Control 45
    The kick-off 47
    Support play 53
    Making space for yourself 59
    The back pass 61
    Attacking the far post 63
    One touch play 64
    The goal keeper in attack 66
    Defeating the full court press 66
    The sixth attacker 73
    Isolating an attacker 75
    Transition and the counter-attack 78
    Set plays from dead ball situations 90
    The power play 97

DEFENSIVE PLAY

- The zone defense 101
- Man for man defense 101
- Defensive tips 102
- Defensive errors 104
- The full court press 104
- Defending against the one-two 107
- One on one tackling 109
- Double teaming 110
- Defending against corner kicks 111
- Defending against the counter-attack 112
- Defending against the power play 113
- The goal-keeper in defense 117
- Substitutions 118
- Formations of play 120
- Training tips 127
- More thoughts on the game 130
- Stretching and cooling down 133
- The professional game 137
- Sample practice session 138

INDOOR SOCCER

TACTICS AND SKILLS

Question: "Do you enjoy playing the indoor game as much as the outdoor game?"

Answer: "Absolutely, I think that it's an exciting game, it's an entertaining game. When you play one and one-half hours of entertaining soccer, I think it's the most exciting game right now in the United States. It's a wonderful one and one-half hours of non stop soccer. You get your money's worth."

Question: "As a player, do you enjoy playing indoors as much as the outdoor game?"

Answer: "Absolutely, I mean when you're getting older, then you need really a skillful game to play and enjoy."

That was **Karl-Heinz Granitza,** perennial all star forward with the **Chicago Sting** of the MISL.

Here's **Mike Dowler,** Goal keeper for the **Tacoma Stars** of the **MISL**.

"Outdoors compared to indoors the goal keeping's a piece of cake, because you have three or four saves, but you're on your toes all the time for the indoor game."

Question: "Do you find the indoor game just crazy or is it lots of fun?"

Answer: "Oh it's lots of fun. For excitement and adventure there's no comparison. The indoor game has more in five minutes than some outdoor games have in a whole game."

It's a fun game. I think it's a great spectator sport. Lots of action, lots of saves, goals. They can see a lot of skill out there. They can see all the action."

From **Jean Willrich:** Midfielder for the **San Diego Soccers** of the **MISL**.

Question: "Is it more fun to play indoor or outdoor soccer?"

Answer: "I think it's very much fun when you play indoors, especially when you have a winning team. Everybody thinks it's very tough, but it's really a simple game."

Question: "Why would you say it's simple?"

Answer: "What we've learned, you drop back with five guys to the first red line when you lose the ball. That means the attackers have ten legs in front of them, plus the goal keeper."

"When the other team attacks with three or four guys, then when you get the ball you can play on them. You defend with one more player than the opponents, and you attack with one more player."

"You must have the right players too, players who play the ball. Then you enjoy it. When you play it up and you get it back one-two, that is fun, that is soccer."

Besides being fun, indoor soccer is great training for certain aspects of the outdoor game. It develops a player's ability to operate at close quarters and under severe pressure. All the physical and mental processes are speeded-up. Individual ball skill is developed along with quick passing decisions. This can only improve a player's effectiveness in the penalty areas outdoors. That's where the goals are scored, and that's what everybody wants to see.

The reduction in size of the playing area eliminates a lot of negative space. There is no place to hide. Every area is vital space and must be contended for. Each player gets to play the ball a lot more, and the action is continuous.

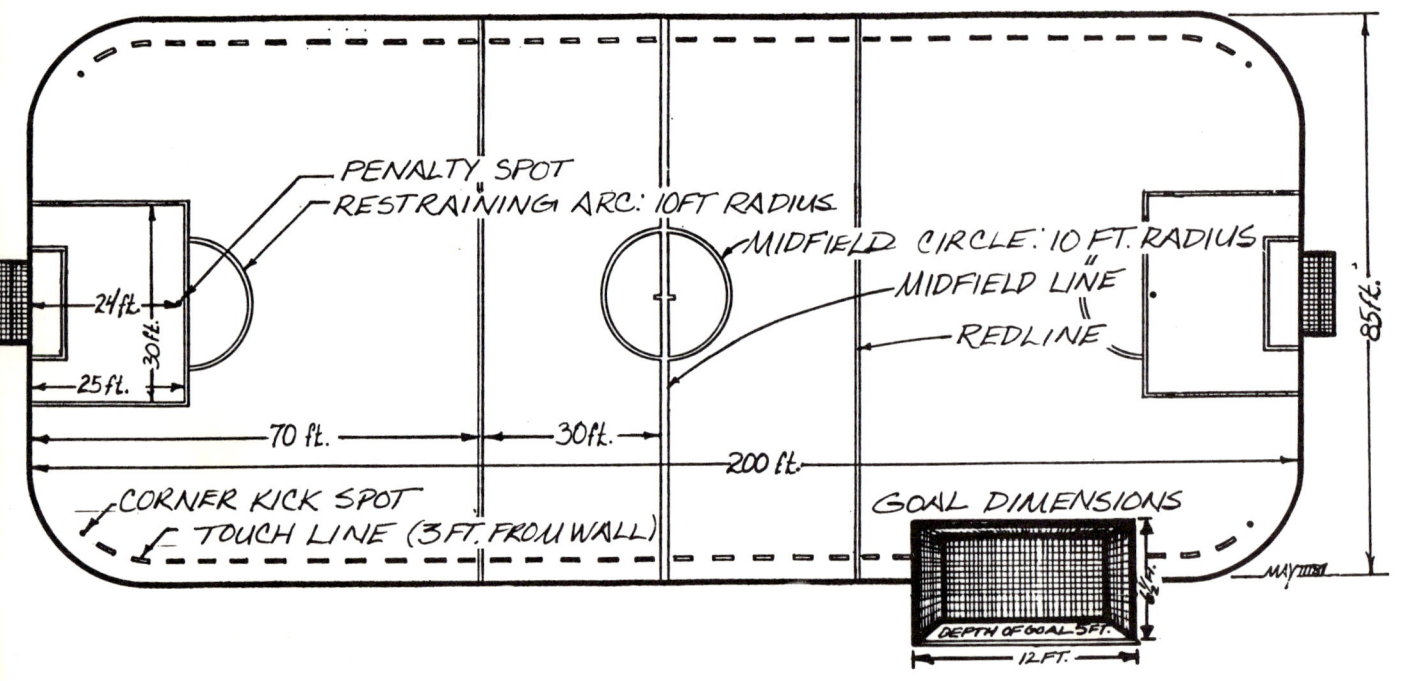

Fig. 1 The playing surface

The major differences between the indoor and outdoor games are:
1. Fewer players indoor: Six a side instead of eleven.
2. The presence of boards surrounding the playing area that open up many new passing moves.
3. The indoor game is divided into four equal periods of play, with rest periods in between.
4. Unlimited substitutions are permitted while the ball is in play.
5. No offside rule is enforced.
6. For various flagrant fouls a player may be sent to the penalty box, leaving his teammates to play a man short.

These special features of Indoor Soccer bring about different tactics than the outdoor game. The old axiom that you can't score without the ball still applies, so the primary effort while attacking is to keep possession of the ball, and the top priority of defense is to get it back as soon as possible.

Keep in mind ball possession should be a positive thing. It shouldn't become so conservative that you fail to score goals. There isn't enough space indoors to try to protect a small lead by negative, defensive possession tactics. You must create scoring chances, and you must take them without hesitation. A three or four goal lead indoors is nothing you can sit on.

From John Best, President of the Tacoma Stars of the MISL.

"My view of indoor soccer is that **possession** is related to **goals** is related to **winning.** You've got to score **goals.**"

The limited space of an indoor soccer court dictates an attacking game, and that's one of the things that make it so exciting.

Bob McNab, Former head coach of the Tacoma Stars indoor team says:

"In essence the game is all about **passing** and **controlling** the ball. Tactics are irrelevant if you can't pass and control the ball; if you can't pass at the correct time, the correct speed, the correct weight. If you can't pass the ball, you don't need any control, because you're never going to get an opportunity to control it."

"So once you've learned to pass it, then you've got to learn to control it. Once you can pass it and control it, then you've got to learn to **support** it. Pass, control, support, those three elements."

The other side of the coin is defensive play, which deals with the ways we can recapture the ball once we've lost it. Positioning, tackling, intercepting, and blocking shots are the skills required here.

Since no strenuous athletic activity should be started without warming up, we'll consider this important preparation and then return to the tactics of indoor soccer.

WARM-UP

A little while back, each sport had its own narrowly conceived method of training. Nowadays we borrow from many sources, searching to improve our physical and mental techniques. This is borrowed from Ballet. For warming-up, every ballet class for hundreds of years has started with deep knee bends. Dancers call them plies. (pronounced plee-ays) They quickly warm-up and stretch the leg muscles and hips in preparation for the strenuous movements that are to follow.

Position #1 Fig. 2

Stand straight, heels touching, arms out to sides, toes turned out as far as possible. Keep the knee right over the foot and your upper body plumb. Bend the knees and sink into a full knee bend until you're sitting on your heels. Do this to a slow count of four. As soon as you reach bottom, start back up to a slow four count. Do three full knee bends, and then with straight legs rise as high as possible on the balls of your feet, as you raise your arms over your head. Hold this position for a slow count of eight. Lower your heels and start the whole sequence over again: three knee bends, rise on toes; three knee bends; rise on toes. Do three or four sets of three knee bends and rise on toes.

Position #1 Fig. 2

Position #2 Fig. 3

Rest briefly, then place your feet in position #2 as shown, and do three or four sets of knee bends in this position, right foot in front, then three or four sets of bends with left foot in front. Turn out your feet only to the extent that you can keep your knees over your ankles as you bend. It's vital that you don't let your knees or ankles roll in. That puts the hip, knee, and ankle out of alignment and strains the joints. Turn out your feet less if necessary. Work on this technique slowly until you get the feel of it. Keep your upper body straight. Don't lean forward. If necessary, hold on to something for balance. Start with arms extended to the side. As your knees bend, lower the arms. As you straighten up, raise arms to the side. As you rise on toes, raise arms overhead and reach. As you lower the heels, lower arms to the side-extended position.

Position #2 Fig. 3

Do as many plies as you like. They are a perfect beginning for any sports activity.

Plies can be done at scattered times throughout your training sessions. They help to keep your leg muscles from tightening up from your strenuous efforts, and they help to develop good knee bend in all your movements. Ballet movement is scientific and anatomically correct, and develops the entire range of bodily movement and strength to it's fullest. It trains the body for **movement** in all possible ways.

If you have the time, you couldn't give yourself any better supplemental training than to take a class or two of ballet training each week, with a **competent** instructor. The benefits can be enormous, especially for older players, or players who took up the game later in life.

The Swinger (Fig. 4) Stand easy with the feet spread comfortably (about 6" apart), arms hanging relaxed at your sides. Rotate the torso, shoulders, and head from side to side in a very easy relaxed manner. The motion starts in the hips; the upper body, arms, and **head** follow. Completely relax the shoulders and arms, letting the arms wrap around your body at each rotation. Allow the opposite heel to lift off the floor on each rotation. No tension in any part of your body. Continue for several minutes.

The Windmill (Fig. 5) Stand easy and comfortably. Rotate one arm from the shoulder in a forward direction ten times. Rotate the same arm in the opposite direction ten times. Repeat the process with the other arm. Relax the shoulders, and allow the arm to swing freely. Don't muscle it around. Let it swing like a stone on the end of a string.

Fig. 4 The Swinger   **Fig. 5 The Windmill**

To stretch or not to stretch, that's the question here. Some say stretch before a work-out, some say after. Some say do both. I think it depends on the individual. Try both ways. If you'd like to stretch at this point, refer to the chapter on cooling down, and execute the stretches shown. Do these quite gently, just enough to loosen up the joints, muscles, tendons and ligaments. Positively no bouncing.

After the stretches, continue the warm-up by executing the movements you would use in a game. Practice your different passes against the wall or to a teammate: inside of the foot, outside of the foot, instep or back heel, on the volley, half volley, etc. Juggle the ball from time to time to develop your touch.

Start all these movements slowly, and gradually increase your speed as you feel your muscles loosening up. By the end of your warm-up you can be doing these things at game speed. Don't take hard shots on goal until you are thoroughly warmed up.

When you are thoroughly warmed-up, practice running backward and sideward in many different patterns and leg cross-overs. Defending and attacking require a lot of backward and sideward movement.

It's important to relax and bend your knees. At some time in each step the heel should contact the floor. Contact of the full surface of the foot gives a solid platform to push off for your next step. It makes for quick, controlled changes of direction.

Try this: Run forward at full speed. Try to stop within a step or two. If you stay up on the balls of your feet, you need quite a few steps to stop your forward motion. Now try to stop, letting your heel strike first, followed by the full surface of the sole of your foot. You find you stop much quicker and with more control. Your knee bends fully, and absorbs your forward motion. Quick starts, quick stops, and quick changes of direction require this deep knee bend and full sole contact with the floor.

Photographs of great players like George Best and Pele just at the moment of changing direction, show how deeply the knees are bent. This permits exaggerated lean of the body from side to side, and makes the fakes and feints more convincing, because you can remain balanced and change direction right up to the last moment. It gives you time to read your opponents reactions, and change your move in midstride.

Do your plies every day to keep your leg muscles strong and supple, and to avoid any soreness that might result if you do them only once or twice a week.

It's foolish to start a match or hard training session without at least fifteen minutes of warm-up. Thirty minutes or more would be much better. Warm-up prepares the joints, muscles, tendons and ligaments for the tremendous loads they carry under game conditions. It adds to their elasticity and greatly diminishes the chances of injury over the years. The older you are the longer the warm-up should be, but slower.

Some players think they can warm-up during the first part of the match, but if the other team is ready to play, they won't permit it. They'll smash in three or four quick goals before the first team is into the game.

The dangers of top speed play without adequate warm-up are too great a risk to take. Warm-up gets your body and mind ready to play.

The importance professionals attach to conditioning, as injury prevention, is shown by the following question and answer.

To **Keith Furphy**, forward for the **Tacoma Stars** of the **MISL**.

Question: "As an attacker, what's the hardest part of the game for you?"
Answer: "Well, indoor soccer is very physical, three games a week, very hard surfaces, and just trying to stay in shape, stay away from **illness** and **injury.** I think that's the hardest part of the game." (Keith Furphy holds the MISL record for consecutive games played, over 230)

EQUIPMENT

Get the best shoes and the best ball you can afford. Your feet bear the full weight of your soccer activity, so no treatment is too good for them. Shoes should fit as snugly as possible without putting any back-pressure on the toes, or preventing the foot from relaxing and spreading out sideways. Try them on wearing the same socks you will wear in a game. There are many shoes designed for artificial turf. Get the shoe that's as light as possible, but supports and protects your foot, and at the same time is the closest thing to being barefoot you can find.

A good ball is gentle to the feet when you kick it. Even fully inflated, it plays easy. It's lively, but well padded and responsive.

Dribbling and kicking depend a lot on "feel". The ball should feel good when you dribble or kick it. Most cheap balls are "dead" if underinflated, and a rock if properly inflated. If your foot unconsciously shies away from striking the ball because it hurts, you'll never develop the "touch" to control it. That "touch" depends on a pleasurable sensation whenever your foot contacts the ball.

When you buy a ball try to test it out before you take it. Bounce it a few times to see if it's lively. It should bounce lightly and with a feeling of life. The individual panels should be padded well enough to make the ball feel good when you juggle it. All balls "play" better as they are broken in, but a good ball feels light and alive, while a bad ball feels dead and heavy even if they both actually weigh the same. A lot of soccer shops are run by people who play the game, and they can usually give you qualified advice about equipment.

-Legend-

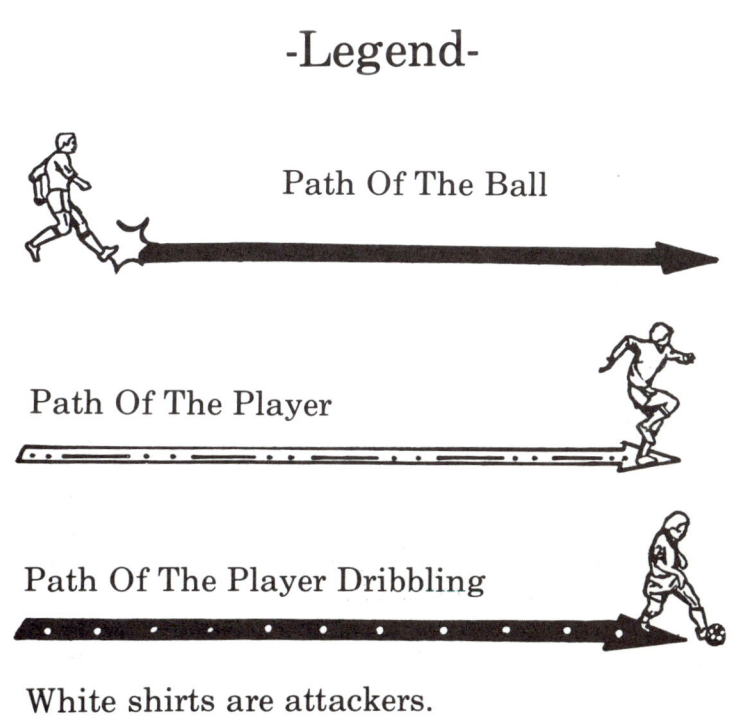

White shirts are attackers.

Black shirts are defenders.

ATTACKING PLAY

PASSING

John Best: "If players can understand the timing of **when** to run as well as **where** to run, then all of a sudden the penny drops, the passing flows, and the team will flow."

Passing the ball involves all of the many kicking techniques. The simplest, easiest, and most accurate kick is the **push pass.** (Fig. 6) Beginners should perfect this kick before any other. Pele used it to take penalty kicks. Stan Stemencovic, one of the most accomplished indoor players of all time, uses this inside of the foot technique, even for shooting the ball.

Intermediate and advanced players should practice it, because it's the basis for the whole passing game.

Fig. 6 The Push Pass

The non-kicking foot strides forward, and is planted pointing toward the target, the heel striking first. The kicking foot is turned out at right angles, and both knees are bent as the kicking foot is drawn back. The ball is struck on the solid part of the inside of the **ankle.** The power applied is controlled by how far you stride, and how high you lift your kicking foot behind you. Most of the time you'll want this pass to stay along the floor. You do this by striding several inches **past** the ball with your non-kicking foot so that your kicking foot meets the ball at the bottom of its swing.

Try to get an experienced player to show you this technique, and check you from time to time. Keep **practicing.** The things to remember are: non-kicking foot **strides** exactly toward the target; the kicking foot is turned out at right angles to it; use enough back lift to generate whatever power is needed; strike the ball with the firm part of the inside of the **ankle.** Practice striking a stationary ball, and then practice hitting a moving ball.

After this pass is mastered, you can gradually move on to the other methods of kicking the ball, the instep kicks. They are much harder to learn, and it's best to learn them slowly from a really accomplished player who knows how to show you the secrets of these techniques.

If you learn the push pass first, and master it, you'll be able to play a credible game of soccer, and the instep kicks will come to you with time. The stretches shown in the cooling down section are all helpful to your kicking techniques because they increase the range of movement of the hips.

Figure 7 shows an excellent passing routine. It's hard to diagram, but study the drawings and keep trying until you get the hang of it. Timing your run to keep the proper spacing from your teammates is the hardest part. Allow the sequence of passes to develop. Strike your passes so they arrive ahead of your teammate, so he can return them in his stride. Hit the passes hard enough to arrive with good timing, but not so hard they are difficult to return. Try to keep the ball on the floor.

This drill is excellent practice for first time passing. It simulates the angles from which you receive passes in a game. It forces you to consider your positioning in the space being used. Continuous use of this drill will help create the instinctive use of the one-two, or wall pass, that is so useful in developing the flow of your passing attack. It will develop your "touch" on the ball and encourage confidence in your one touch passing.

Continuous One Touch Passing Drill (Fig. 7)

"A"
    (a) Player #2 makes his run
    (b) Player #1 passes to Player #2
    (c) Players #1 and #3 make their runs.

"B"
    (a) Player #2 receives the ball and plays it first time to Player #3
    (b) Player #1 makes his run.

"C"
    (a) Player #3 receives the ball and plays it first time to Player #1
    (b) Players #2 and #3 make their runs.

Continue for as long as desired.

Possible variations:

    1. Reverse direction
    2. All passes to be made with the right foot
    3. All passes with the left foot
    4. All passes with the inside of the foot
    5. All passes with the outside of the foot
    6. All passes on the volley

Fig. 7 Continuous Passing Drill

Fig. 7 "A" **Fig. 7 "B"** **Fig. 7 "C"**

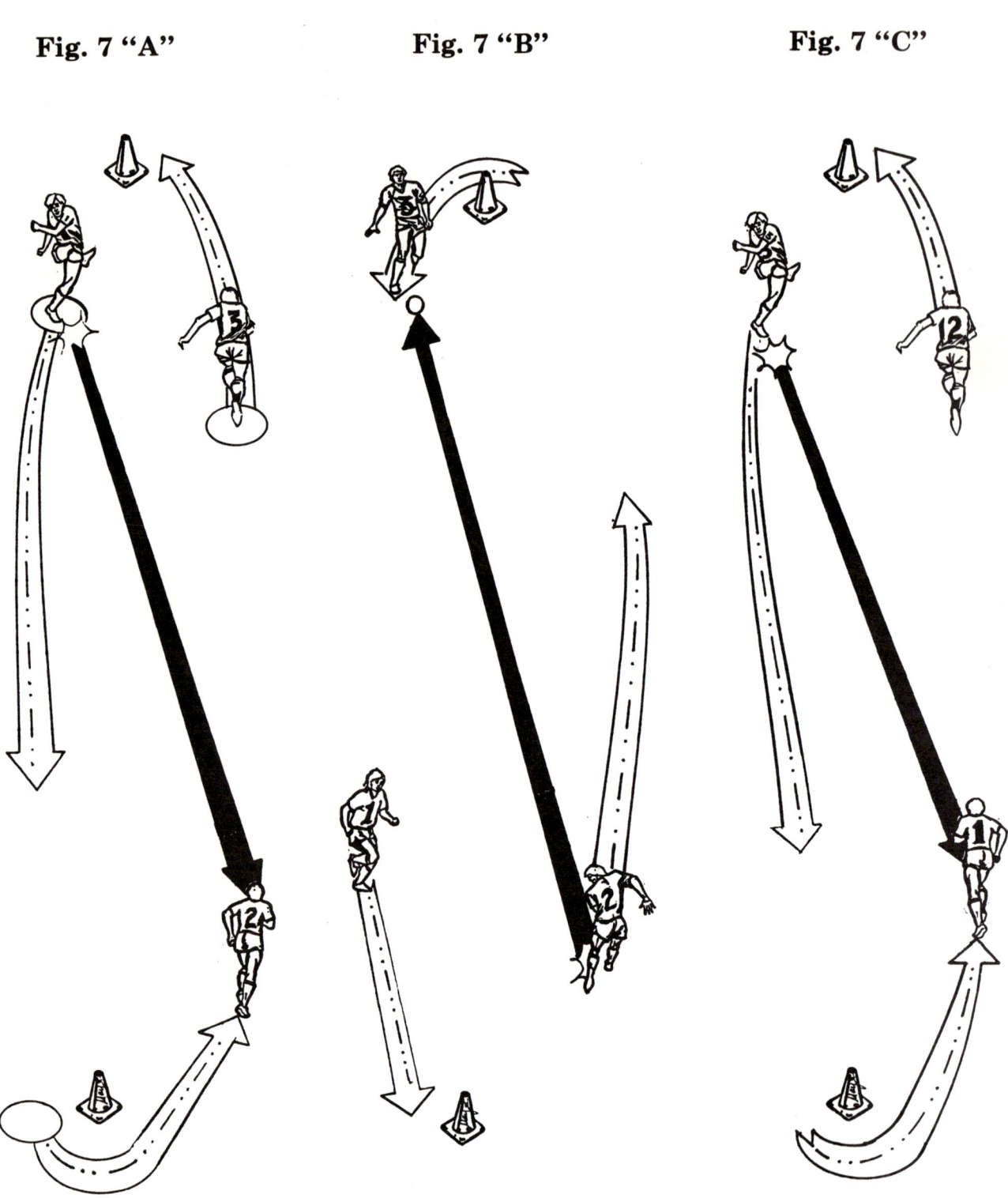

Passing Drill (Fig. 8)

(a) Player #5 dribbles the ball a short distance, calls the name of player #8, passes the ball to him, and continues his run until he occupies #8's position.

(b) Player #8 dribbles the ball a short distance, calls the name of player #3, passes the ball to him, and continues his run until he occupies #3's position.

(c) The drill continues on in this manner.

This drill emphasizes picking out your pass early, communicating with your teammates, and running into space vacated by another player.

Use any number of players and enough balls to keep the action going. As you add additional balls to the drill, it becomes clear the quality and timing of the passes is critical. If you don't use your eyes and don't direct the passes with accuracy and the proper speed, you will have a comedy of confusion. This drill quickly accustoms the players to each others' reactions, and introduces new players into the group through the process of calling out names.

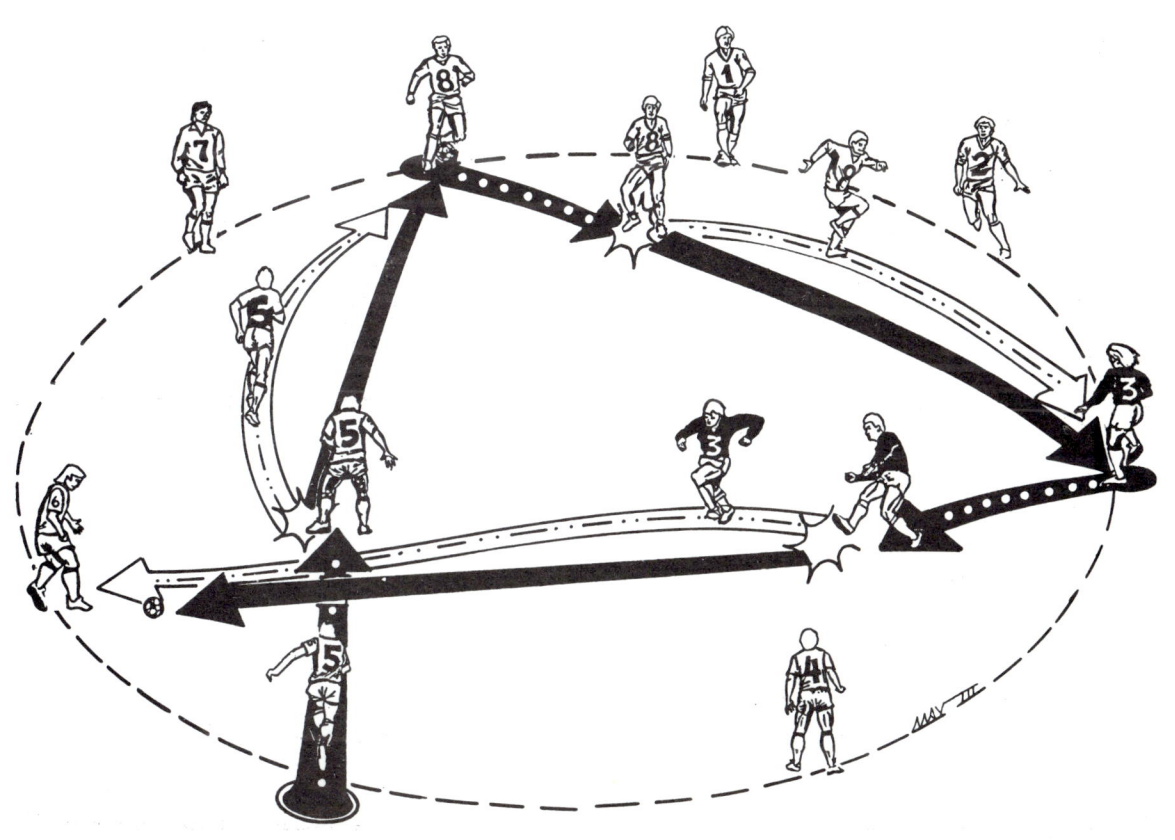

Fig. 8

In all soccer play, passing, control, making runs, and support are involved. To be successful, a team has to combine the correct execution of these principles, and realize how they are interdependent on each other.

To be effective, a pass has to arrive where you want it, when you want it. It has to be timed well and struck well. Your eyes and brain help accomplish this. You have to play with your eyes up off the floor. As you dribble, you look up between touches of the ball to take in the positions of the other players. Just before you strike a pass, you look up. Your brain records a picture of the situation, and as you look down to strike the pass, the image remains in your head, and the calculations of weight, distance, and angle of direction are made, and the pass is played. The more you can keep your eyes off the floor, the better you can play the game. This is one of the hardest things to learn for most soccer players. Therefore it's worth lots of work.

Practice, practice, practice until you are completely at home receiving and passing the ball, then the tactical solutions to the game will come to you much easier.

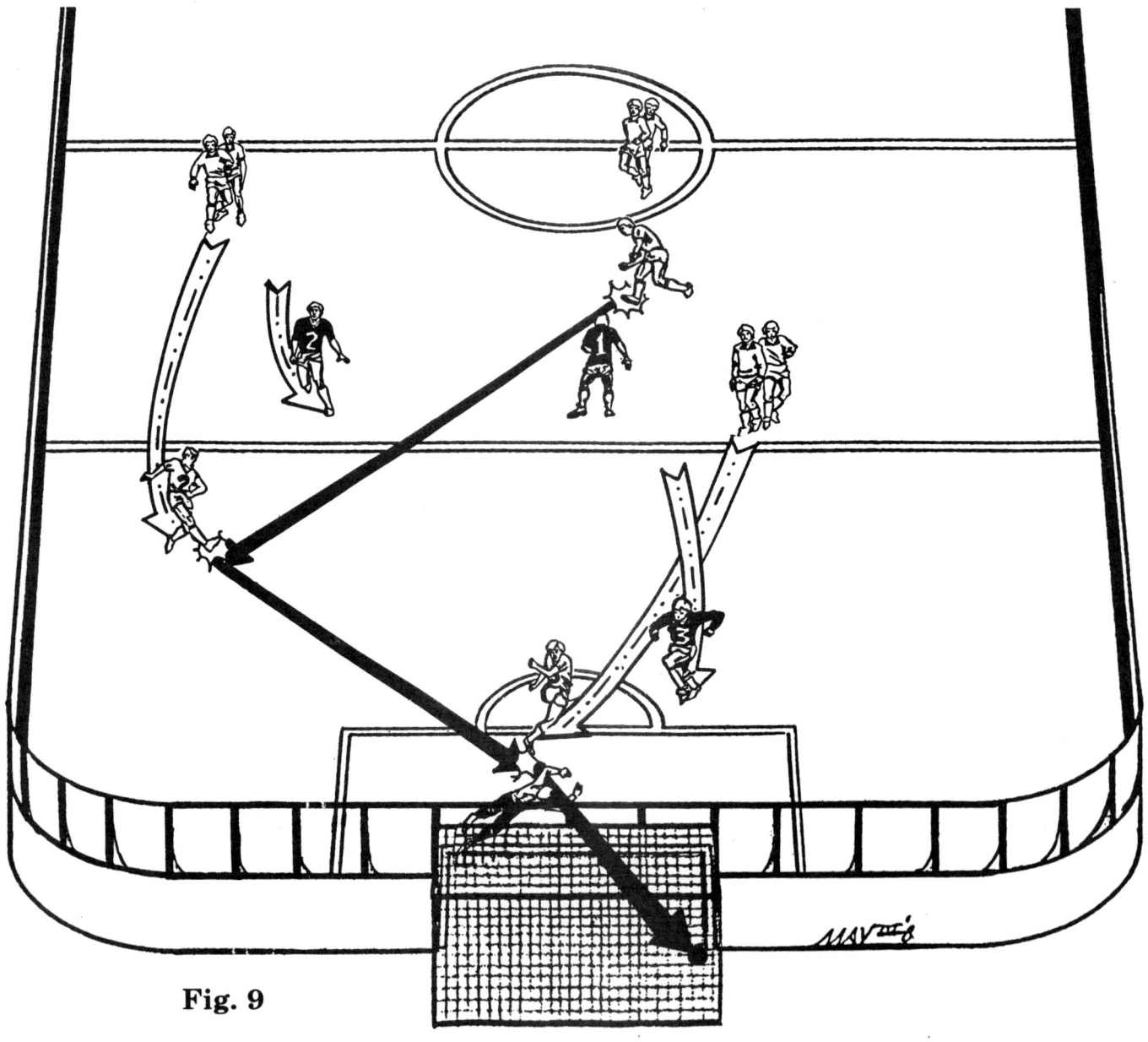

Fig. 9

PLAYING THE BALL INTO SPACE (Fig. 9)

(a) As attacker #2 sprints past defender #2, attacker #1 plays a pass ahead of him, so that he can receive it in his stride.
(b) Attacker #3 times his run to that of attacker #2, so that he can receive in his stride the pass played by attacker #2.

(c) Attacker #3 receives the pass from attacker #2, and takes a shot on goal.

The passes are played into space **behind** the defenders for the attackers to run onto. It's important that the player receiving the pass doesn't run too soon and have to wait for the ball, giving his defender a chance to recover. The defenders are forced to turn and chase the ball, giving the attackers a chance to gain a step and reach the ball first. Timing the pass to the run of the receiver is the key to success.

Use as a drill with passive defenders at first, then the defenders can become more active, but they should allow the play to work. They should turn and follow the ball but not prevent the passes from being made.

All the plays shown in the book can be made into drills in this way. That gives the players a chance to **repeat** the action often enough to recognize the various situations when they come up in a game. **Repetition** is the great **teacher.**

Players often run too soon for fear they won't be seen, and won't get the ball. By practicing the passing plays, passer and receiver will each become conscious of his functions. When the **timing** of the run and the pass has been rehearsed a number of times, the runner becomes confident he will receive the ball. An **understanding** is built between passer and runner.

Look for space to play the ball into, then for the man to run onto it. If you run too soon, you have to wait for the ball, and the opponents can close down, making further progress difficult.

Practice playing the ball into space and letting your teammate find it. That way you encourage proper movement, and the game begins to flow.

Relax, relax. All body movement originates in the area from the hips to the solar plexus. Tension in this area interferes with the fluid movement needed to execute athletic techniques. When you run, think of your lower torso starting the movement. Your legs and feet will automatically support you, and your knees will bend naturally to give you smooth, balanced movement. Keep the muscles of the feet and ankles at ease, with your weight well balanced over your ankles.

Practice running like this whenever you get a chance. Do it without a ball at first, and then do your dribbling moves while remembering your running style. It's hard to correct flaws in your running style, so don't expect miracles. Just gradually work on it. The main thing is to concentrate on relaxing the lower torso, and avoid getting your weight too far forward. You should stay balanced right over your ankles.

PRACTICING USING THE DIAGRAMS

For practice purposes, coaches and players can take any of the attacking or defensive plays shown here, and make a drill out of them.

Just group several players at each station of the diagram, and then make a continuous drill out of it as shown in diagram. (Fig. 9)

The way to understand these or any plays is to repeat them over and over as a drill, then gradually you will react to the situation when it comes up in a game. You will be able to recognize when a certain play should be used. It will give organization to your team.

To keep the players' attention from lapsing, try to have most drills end with a shot on goal. Simulate game conditions as much as possible. Start by **walking** through the play without the ball, then walk through it with the ball. Go through it at a slow run. Keep increasing the speed until it's at game pace. This way people will get to understand the **timing** required of the runs and the passes. Now introduce defenders into the attacking plays as inactive stationary posts. Next let the defenders move with the play but not tackle. Remember, the defenders will know exactly what the attackers are going to do, so at critical stages of the play the defenders should allow the play to work. They should apply pressure, but allow the play to flow.

Good teams aren't making up the game as spontaneously as it seems. They are reacting to situations they have practiced many times. This way you develop a **pattern** of play that everyone on your team is familiar with. Your battle plan takes form, and your positioning and the **timing** of your runs begin to have meaning for you and your teammates.

Simplify your game by taking it apart and analyzing it. Practice the individual parts, and then blend them together for your final result.

These diagramed plays and drills are the A B C's of your system of play. Without them your movement is largely extemporaneous and often self destructive. They're building blocks. Practice them until you can perform them consistenty, and you'll find your game gains form and structure, your confidence in your method grows, and things begin to work for you.

Indoor soccer may look spontaneous, but it's not. It's just like most other games. You're only successful if you execute basically sound tactical moves with skill and presicion, and that takes practice.

When you practice correct moves, your understanding of the game expands immediately, and your enjoyment along with it. Everyone likes to feel he is doing something right. When you put together all the different plays and drills, you're putting together a tactical system that will make you more successful. It takes less effort to do it right, than to randomly kick and chase the ball. It gives enormous satisfaction to make the ball work for you, rather than the other way around.

It's surprising how quickly a team can pull itself together, when they practice some meaningful drills that are game-related. The repetitive nature of a drill quickly increases the accuracy of your passes, the cleanness of your trapping, and the timing of your runs. In a game, everything has to work right the first time, You can't call back that bad pass. In a drill, you are constantly correcting everything, and presently you can do it right the first time.

It's a mistake ever to think you are beyond the stage where you need to execute drills. The higher your skill level, the more difficult you can make the drills. Vladimir Horowitz, world celebrated pianist, although well past the average retirement age, is still giving concerts to critical acclaim. He's the first to admit that without his daily practice of scales (drills), he would be totally unable to perform at concert level.

If the great ones need their daily practice, we recreational athletes should take note.

To Keith Furphy, of the Tacoma Stars of the MISL.

Question:"Are there any set things you practice?"

Answer: "Well, there are a lot, and a lot of that comes with familiarity with the players you work with. If you get into a team with twelve new guys, you'll have a hard time trying to play set plays and different moves in the general course of the game. You will have plenty of set plays at corner kicks and free kicks, because you can work on them in practice; but in the general course of the game, it's quite different when you don't know the players."

"I was at Cleveland for four years, and played with Craig Allen for three of them, and we had tremendous understanding. We had a lot of set plays we would use in the flow of the game. They may seem to have been off the cuff, but they weren't. They were definitely plays that we had worked on together after training, where he makes a certain run, and I play the ball a certain way. There are all kinds of stuff you can work on."

Defending is largely reacting. Attacking requires initiative, and the more set combinations you have, the easier attacking becomes.

KEEP-AWAY

The game of keep-away develops all the fundamentals of passing, control, and support. You can vary the number of players and the number of touches allowed according to the skill level and experience of the players.

(Fig. 10) Beginners and inexperienced players can start with four attackers in a ten or twelve yard square against one defender in the middle.

The idea is for the four attackers to pass the ball among themselves while preventing the lone defender from intercepting it. Any number of touches are allowed and the roughly square shaped formation should be maintained by the attackers.

The defender will have to work very hard in order to capture the ball, if the attackers **move** about off the ball, and pass with quickness and precision. This exercise closely simulates the real game, and teaches the attackers to choose their pass in advance and control the ball quickly to prevent the defender from getting it.

The attackers have to pick out their pass, make the pass, and **move** to a new position to be available for a return pass. This is the whole idea of soccer in a nutshell. Find the open man, make the pass, then **move** to another open space for the return pass.

The attackers forming the square do not stand still. They keep moving in relation to the ball and the defender, so as to maintain constantly open **passing lanes** among themselves. The pattern of their **movement** should retain the roughly square shape.

The **movement** of the people who don't have the ball makes prolonged possession of the ball possible. That's called running off the ball, and it's the basis for all attacking moves in soccer.

Never take this drill lightly. Work hard at it, and the results will show in a real game.

The purpose of any drill is to have it work, to have the players successful in executing it. For instance in keep-away, if the four attackers can't maintain possession of the ball for reasonable lengths of time, then use five, six, seven or eight in a circle, until they are successful. Simplify the drill until it works. You learn nothing from a drill you can't complete. This applies to any drill you attempt.

Conversely, as the players' skills increase, reduce the numbers to three attackers and one defender. Then two attackers and one defender. Keep the action within the ten or twelve yard square area. When the defender captures the ball, or the ball is misplayed out of the area, the player who misplayed the ball becomes the defender.

Just as the drill's difficulty is increased by reducing the number of attackers, it can also be made more difficult by decreasing the size of the playing area. Try to match the degree of difficulty to the skill level of the players.

This drill can become a furious, hilarious game. It's really fun, and should never become a dull routine.

To maintain these favorable formations and movements, your head has to constantly swivel to take in the changing positions of your teammates and the defenders.

While the keep-away game is great training for the attackers, it's also excellent training for the defenders.

As a defender you quickly learn that you will do an awful lot of running without touching the ball, if you don't start to use your head. You have to watch closely the passes being made, and try to anticipate when you will get a favorable angle for an interception or a tackle.

Be ready to pounce on the ball whenever a sluggish or misdirected pass is played. Learn to sense when you have maneuvered yourself into an advantageous position, and can force a mistake by the attackers. Most of all you have to work almighty hard, or you're going to be in the middle a long time. Remember we're only defending because we have to, and we want to get that ball back as soon as possible.

Fig. 10

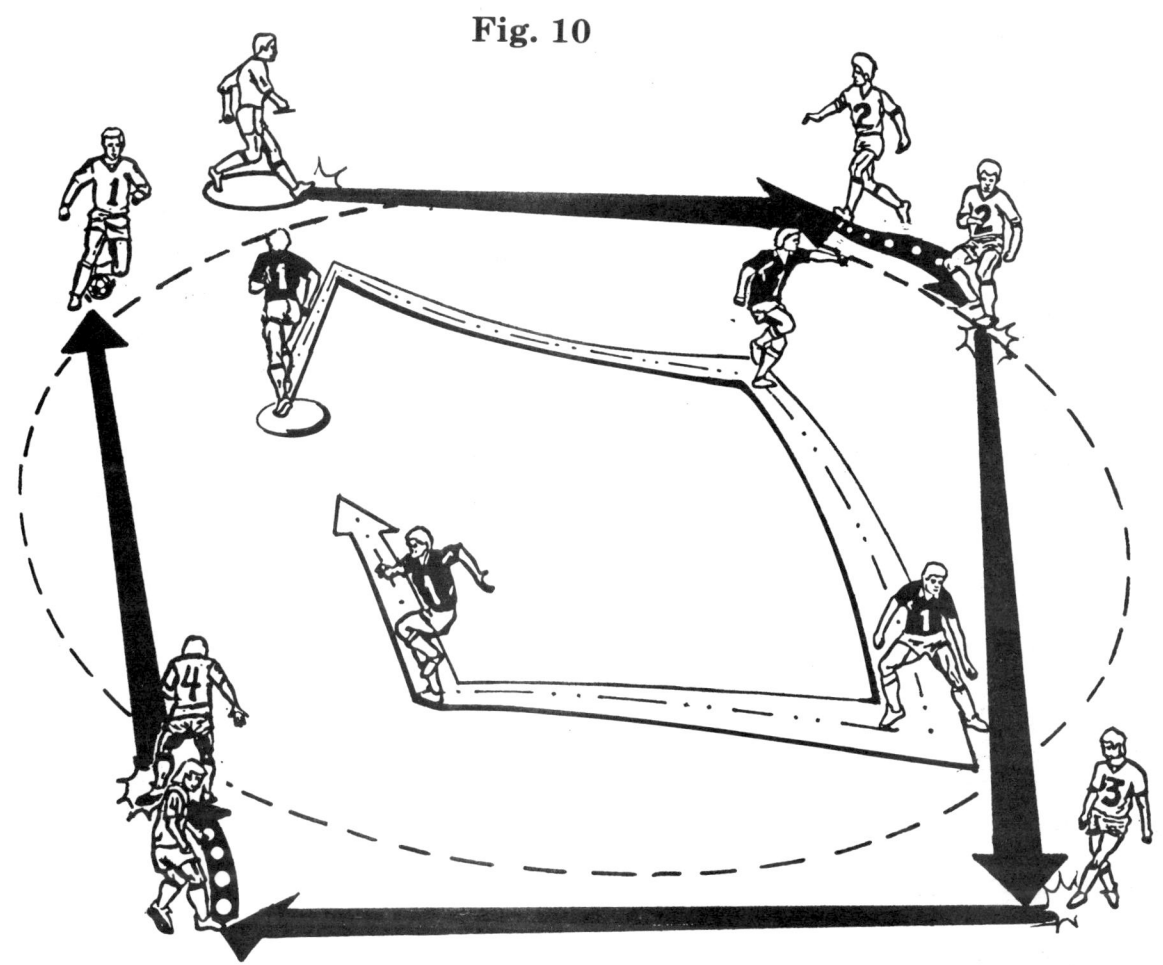

KEEP-AWAY (Fig. 10)

Four against One: For beginning and less experienced players. Start with a ten to twelve yard square-circular area.

> (a) White #1 plays a pass to White #2.
> (b) White #2 moves toward White #1 to make it easier for the passer to find him with the ball.
> (c) White #2 dribbles back a short distance to open a little space for his pass to White #3.
> (d) White #3 does the same and then sends his pass to White #4.
> (e) Because of the quick, crisp passes and the **movement** of the white attackers, Black defender #1 runs futilely chasing the ball with no success.

The sooner the attackers play the ball, the farther away the defender will be, and the more passing options the man on the ball will have. If they play the ball **early** and **accurately**, the defender has no chance to tackle it, and the attackers can easily run his legs off.

This principle of playing the ball **early** should be carried over to the actual game. Good **movement** gives you passing options that you must use, before the defenders close them down. When the pass is open, make it. Don't wait until the defender's challenge closes down most of your space to play it.

Fig. 11

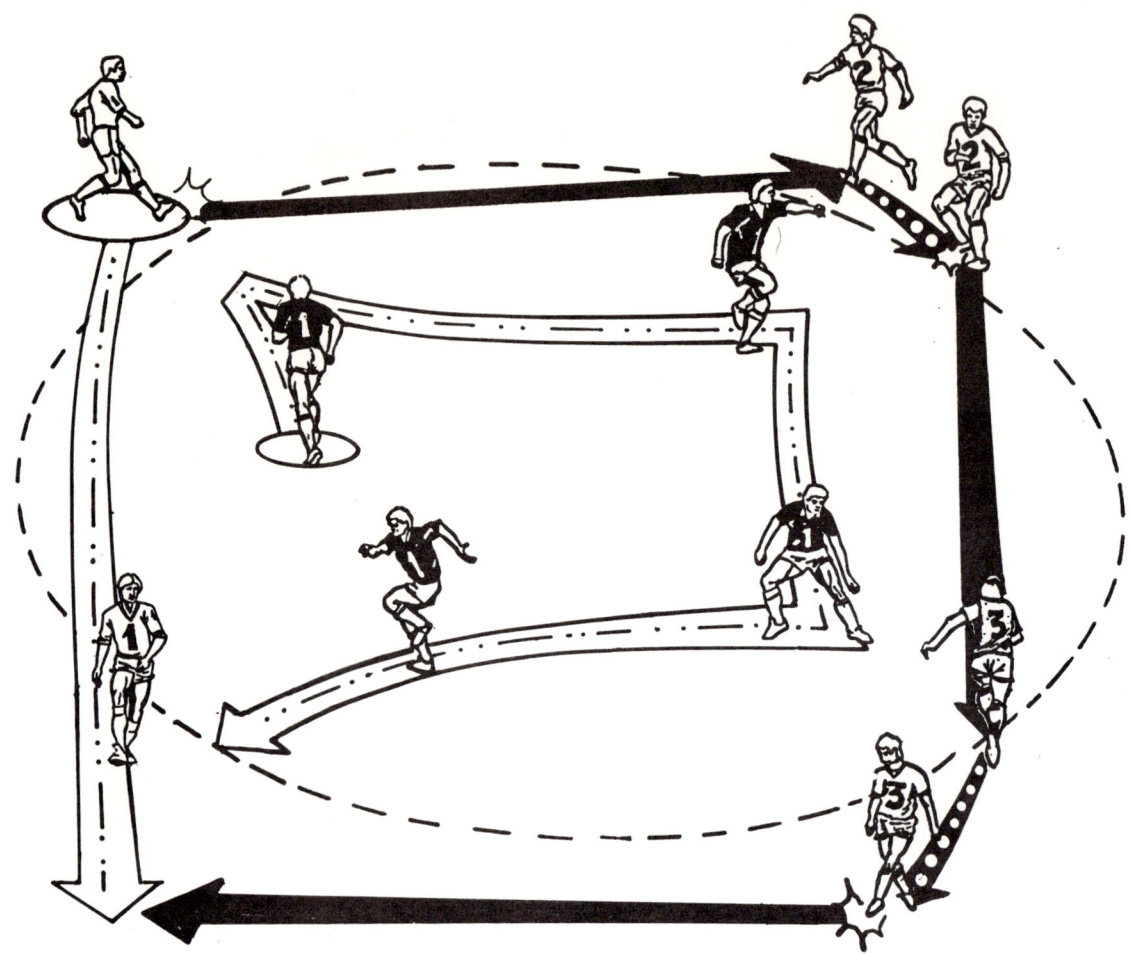

When the attackers can keep the ball away from the defender consistently, gradually reduce the size of the area until it becomes harder for the attackers to keep possession.

KEEP-AWAY (Fig. 11)

Three against One: For more advanced players.

(a) White #1 passes to White #2.
(b) White #2 passes to White #3.
(c) White #1 runs to a new position to improve the passing angle for him to receive the ball from White #3.
(d) The defender Black #1 has to chase the ball trying to hurry the attackers into a mistake.

With one less attacker, they have to run more off the ball in order to keep possession.

When the attackers can keep lengthy possession of the ball, gradually reduce the size of the area, or restrict the attackers to three, two, or one touch.

Fig. 12

KEEP-AWAY (Fig. 12)

Two against One: For advanced players.

>(a) White #2 makes a run to free himself to receive a pass from White #1.
>(b) White #1 passes to White #2, and then runs to a new position to receive a return pass from White #2.
>(c) Black #1 has to chase the ball, and try to force a mistake by the White players.

Attacker #1 must pass and immediately run to an open area to receive a return pass, before the defender can close down on his teammate. Because of the **movement** needed to get free, the man with the ball will be playing it into space for his teammate to run on to, rather than directly to his teammate.

In this situation it's continuous pass and **move**, or you're going to lose the ball. This routine is very strenuous and can only be practiced for short intervals, but it really teaches how to exploit 2 on 1 situations, and that's a basic tactic in any soccer game.

Fig. 13

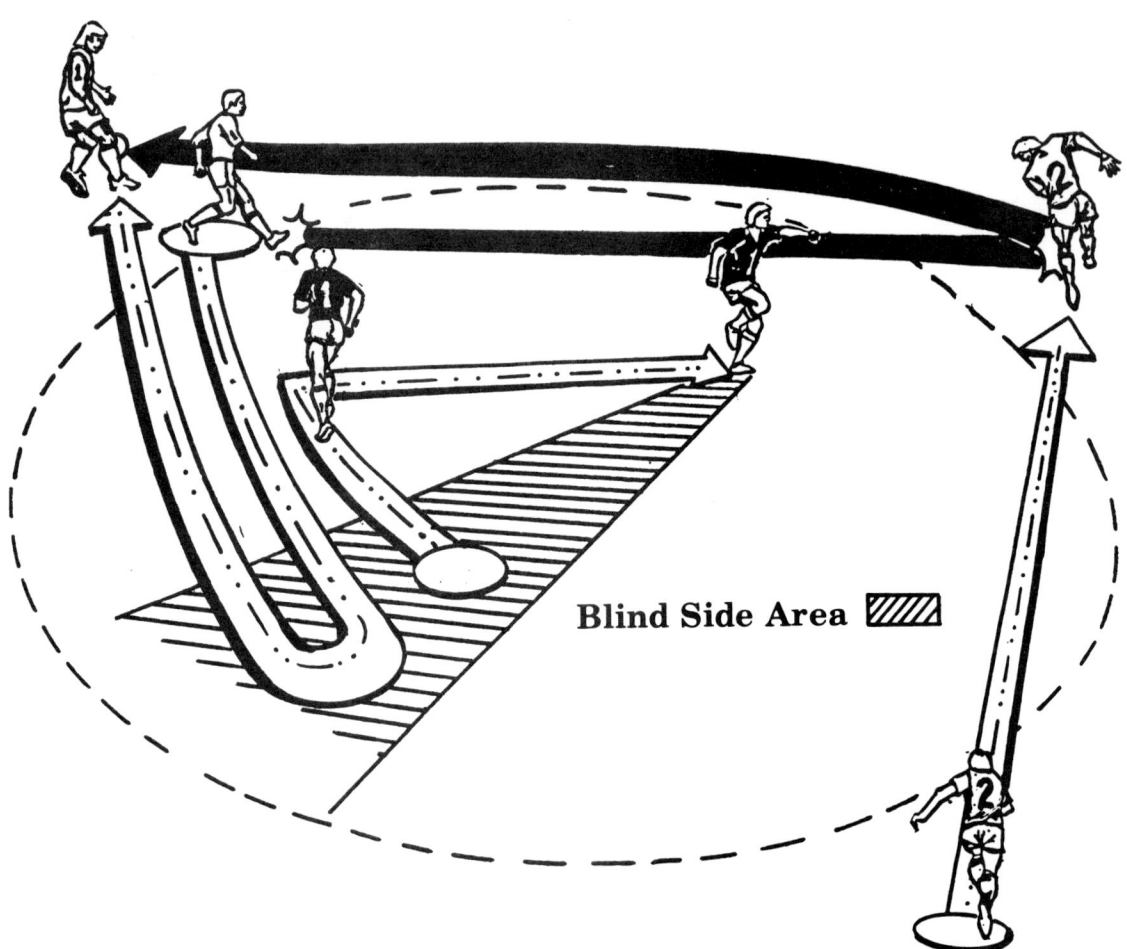

Blind Side Area

KEEP-AWAY (Fig. 13)

Two against One: For advanced players.

(a) White #2 makes a run to get free to receive a pass from White #1.
(b) White #1 passes to White #2, then makes a run to get clear for a return pass.
(c) White #1 makes his run to the defender's blind side area, then checks back to his original spot to receive the return pass.

The man with the ball has to make feints to get the defender going the wrong way, and then make his pass. Attackers have to make false runs to elude the close attention of the defender.

To do this, you have to get behind the defender and on to his blind side. When you can no longer see his eyes, he can no longer see you. That's when you make your final move. Getting on the defender's blind side means he can't see you and the man with the ball at the same time. That's your advantage. It takes close cooperation between the two attackers to time their runs and passes correctly. When you work at this routine for a while, you realize why the professional indoor players only enter the game for 2 to 2½ minute segments. They run a lot, and they run hard.

Fig. 14 "A"

KEEP AWAY: TWO AGAINST FIVE (Fig. 14)

Fig. 14 "A"
(a) White #2 plays a pass to White #1.
(b) Black #1 closes down on White #1, and slightly left to cut off the passing lanes to White #4 and #5.
(c) Black #2 moves to a position where he can best cut off a pass to White #2, #3 or #4.

In this drill the attackers, by constant movement and playing the ball **early,** try to keep the ball out of reach of the defenders. The defenders, by hard work and astute positioning, try to isolate the ball and steal it from the attackers. This type of action goes on continuously in any indoor soccer match.

When playing two defenders, you have to use teamwork to capture the ball. One player closes down on the ball and the other moves to cut off the passing lanes that are left. As the attackers pass the ball around, the defenders keep shifting their positions so that the one nearest the ball closes down while his partner covers him and cuts off the lanes.

It's cat and mouse and as much mental as physical, with a lot of feinting and faking going on, as the attackers try to keep their passes flowing, and the defenders try to dispossess them.

Fig. 14 "B"
(a) By moving, White #3 finds space to receive the ball from White #1.
(b) Being nearest the ball, Black #2 closes down on White #3 and in a position to cut off a pass to White #1 and #2.
(c) Black #1 moves to a covering position to cut off passing lanes to White #4, #5 and #1.

Fig. 14 "B"

Fig. 14 "C"
(a) The positioning of Black #1 and #2 forces a pass to White #4.
(b) Black #1 and #2 pounce in to attempt a tackle.
(c) White #2 moves in support of White #4 trying to give him some place to play the ball.

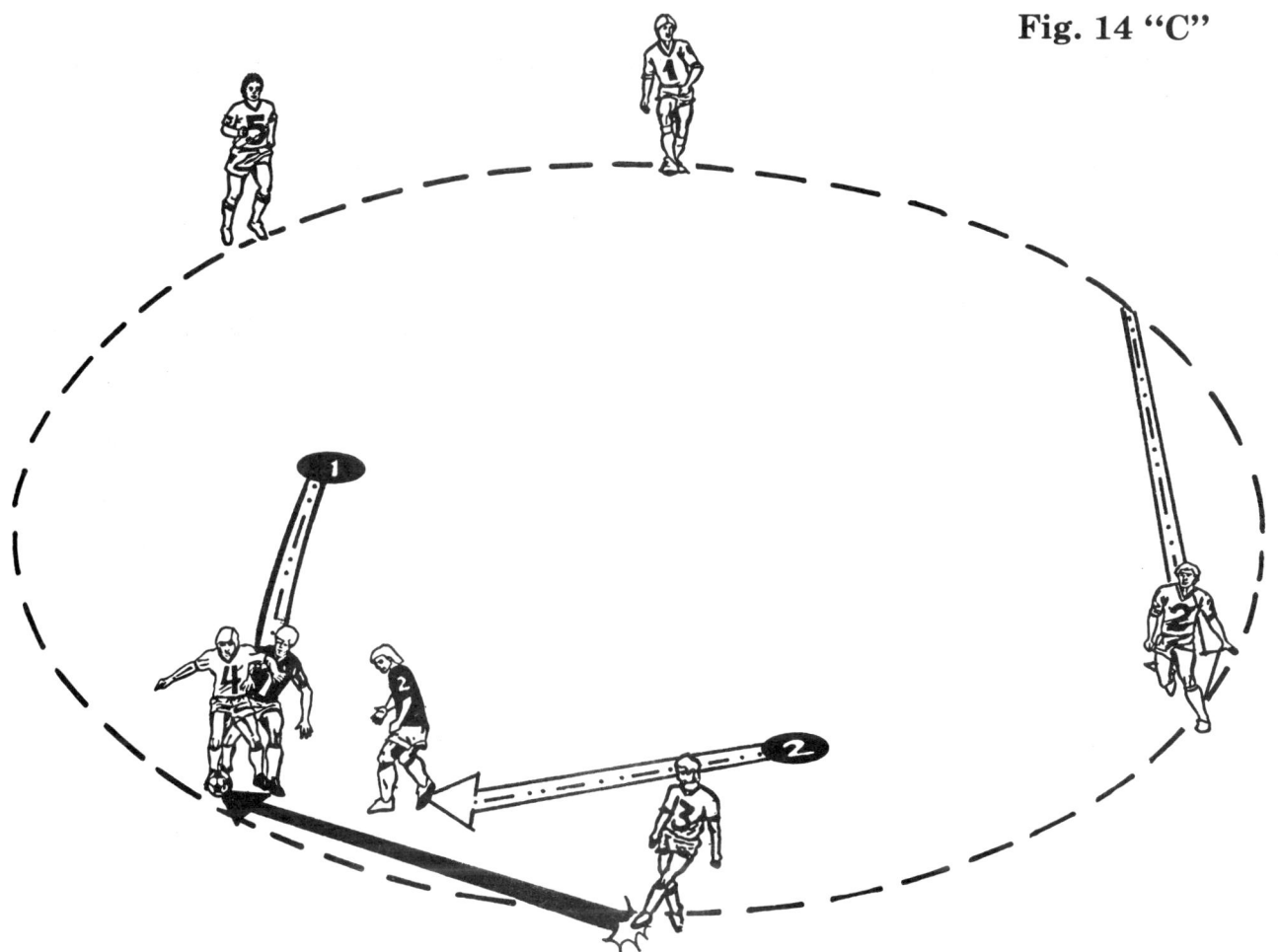

Fig. 14 "C"

Variations that can be used:

    1. Restrict attackers to two touches, then one touch.
    2. Require the ball to be played in the air on the volley or half-volley.
    3. Require the ball to be headed every third or fourth touch. This means one player will have to lift the ball with his foot in order for a teammate to head it.
    4. Make up your own rules according to the number of players and their degree of skill.

Consideration of tactics is pointless without the basic skills needed to carry them out. The constant practice of the basic methods of striking the ball, dribbling, passing and trapping is absolutely indispensable to your understanding of tactics.

Work out the various ways you can play keep-away. Never tire of this kind of mini-game.

Make quality time of your training, by practicing game-related routines such as keep-away, rather than just aimlessly kicking the ball around. Gradually you will make friends with the ball, and enjoy the game more and more.

Get in as many small sided scrimmages as you can: two on two; three on three; four on four. Use small goals and shorter fields. This type of activity is fun, but it also improves your dribbling, passing, and trapping skills, and makes you **want** the ball while you are playing.

Aside from the counterattack break-away, a full size game of indoor soccer is a continuous game of keep away as you move toward the goal and then take shots.

Here's how you can move the ball towards the goal by maintaining moving triangular groups of players. (Fig. 15) The groups of three players keep up the movement within the triangle necessary to interpass the ball, just as in your keep-away drills, while the triangle itself moves toward the goal.

The open triangles serve the purpose of keeping space around each player so that he has room to receive the ball and pass it. By staying **spread out like this, you can help to keep the game one on one.** It makes the defenders work hard and prevents them from double teaming the man with the ball.

OPEN TRIANGLE (Fig. 15)

This spread formation allows maximum freedom to move, pass, or receive the ball.

Practice to develop this sense of open space in your attacking movements.

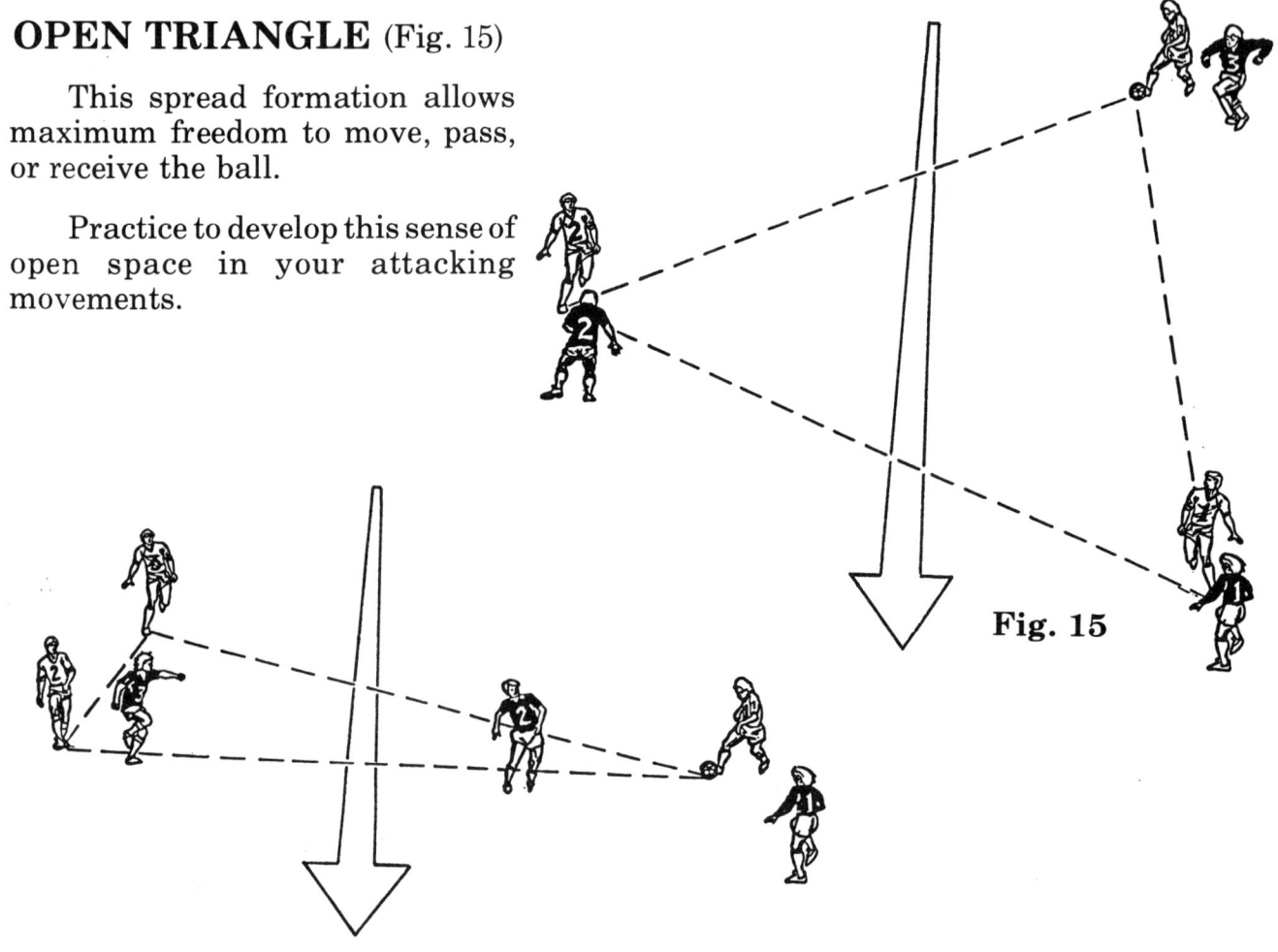

Fig. 15

Fig. 16

CLOSED OR FLAT TRIANGLE (Fig. 16)

Assume white #1 has the ball. With White #2 and #3 so close together, Black #3 can mark them both, leaving Black #2 free to double team the ball carrier and close off the passing lanes.

This is a common positional mistake among inexperienced players. The attackers (White) have to move quickly out of this confining position to more open areas.

MAINTAINING OPEN TRIANGLES (Fig. 17)

By their movement the attacking players keep open configurations, maintain good passing triangles, and are able to support each other as they move toward goal.

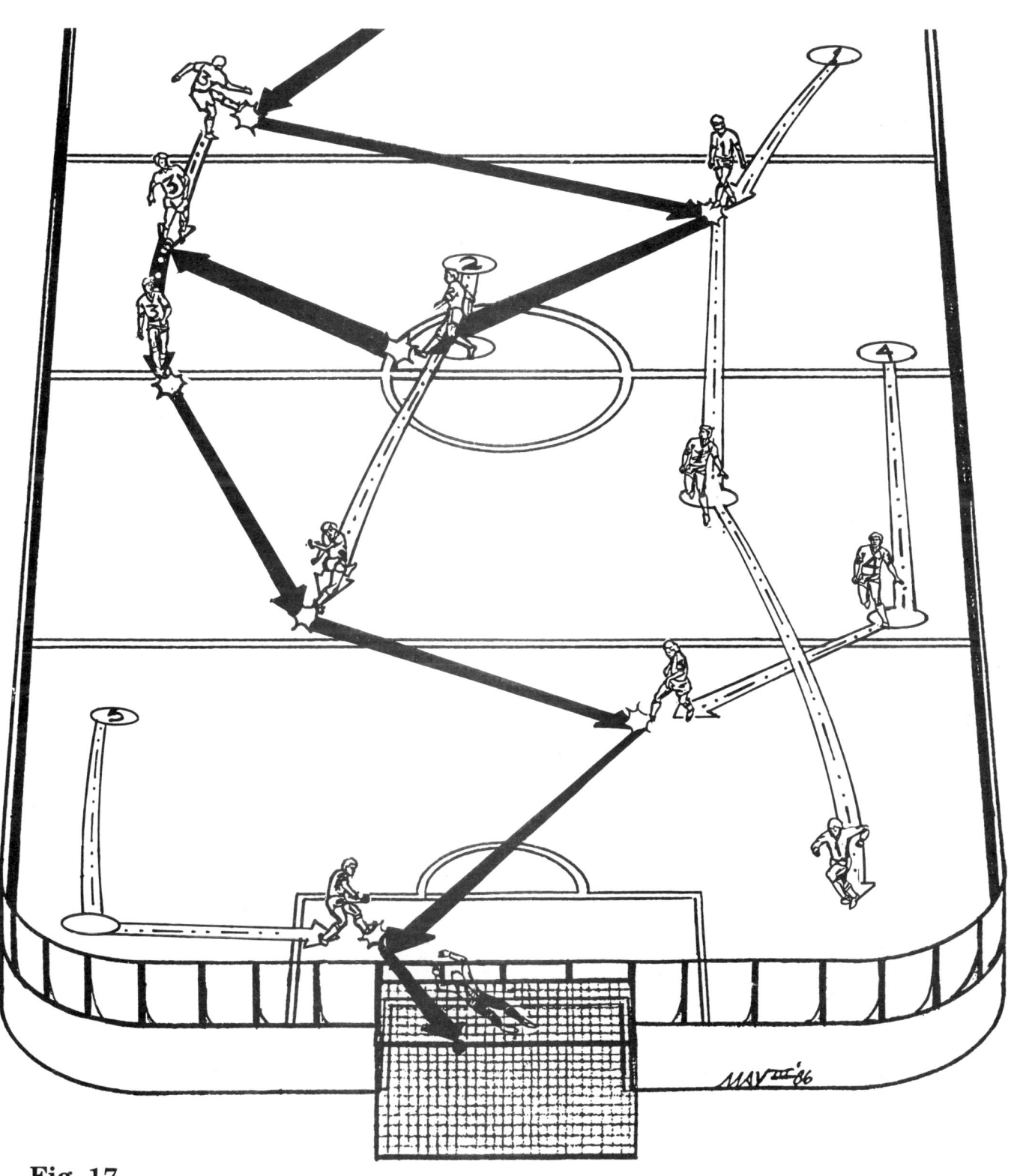

Fig. 17

DRIBBLING THE BALL

In most ball sports, your feet and legs transport you from place to place, while your hands play the ball. In soccer, you're asking your feet and legs to transport you, and at the same time to play the ball. They already know how to transport you, but asking them to play the ball too is like asking one hand to pat your head while the other is rubbing your stomach. It can be done, but it takes practice.

The secret of dribbling is to maintain your stride and balance and weight shift, while touching the ball along, and moving it from side to side, while avoiding tacklers. For practice purposes, you can lay out an obstacle course, composed of cones, shoes, jackets, etc. Place them in random positions a few steps apart from each other. They represent defenders. Plan a path through them that you would like to take. Without the ball, walk this path, visualizing the defending players.

Now at a slow speed, run this path. Continue running the path at increasing speeds. Go back to the walking pace and dribble the ball through the path at a walk. Gradually increase your running and dribbling speed until you can negotiate the path at game speed.

It will take constant practice to run this obstacle course successfully with the ball under control. Try to find an accomplished dribbler who will show you the various weight shifts and other tricks required to make the sudden changes of direction that make dribbling moves succeed. Change the arrangement of the obstacles from time to time.

This sort of solitary practice will gradually teach your legs to carry you from place to place, and play the ball at the same time. Eventually you will be able to make these dribbling moves against a real opponent, but that will only come when they become an automatic, intuitive process. Don't be discouraged. In time you'll do it, and enjoy one of the most fun things in soccer, beating an opponent one on one.

In dribbling you have to run around the ball from side to side in order to change direction. Most people let the ball get too far out in front, and then try to change its direction by reaching for it.

Instead, you have to stay balanced and on top of the ball, so you can change its direction without reaching too far for it. It helps to run flat footed with the heel striking the floor first and the **knees well bent and relaxed.** This way you can keep your balance and change direction more easily.

Try looking at the obstacles (defenders) and playing the ball by your peripheral vision. Also, you have to look up from time to time to see what's ahead. Keep at it 'till you can beat little kids, your dog, assorted furniture, etc. and finally determined defenders.

Every time you see a ball at your feet, wherever you are, slay a few dragons (beat a few imaginary defenders). Your fun in the game increases in direct proportion to your ability to **dribble past your opponents.**

Even professionals can extend their careers by adding to their dribbling and control moves. What might be lost, over the years, in sheer physical force, can be offset by acquiring new techniques. The increased balance, subtlety, and refinement of your play buys fractions of seconds of time for you in your maneuvering with the ball.

If you seriously study the great ball handlers, you can pick up their secrets, and add some of them to your own skills. Never be satisfied with what you can do now. There is an infinite world of movement just ahead of you at all times. Tune into it and keep **expanding** your capabilities. By persistence you can secure the secrets that are just beyond your grasp. Each new move leads to another. The more you know, the easier it gets to know more.

One of the veteran pitchers in the 1986 World Series admitted that when someone showed him how to throw the fork ball sinker, it renewed his career, and brought him out of relative obscurity into national prominence. Like a dancer who adds to his repertoire of steps, we can learn from those who can already do it.

THE CHANGE OF PACE

Change of pace means altering your speed from slow to fast or vice-versa. Some people run at the same speed all the time. It's easy to play against them, because once you figure out their speed, you can make one adjustment, and then you pretty much have them pegged.

Other players can change their speed at will, making it very difficult to mark or tackle them. If you have the ball and are attacking an opponent, start at him slowly or at medium speed. When he closes down on you, push the ball past him six feet or so, and quickly step around him with a burst of speed that takes you a step or two past him, and you are off to the races.

The same thing applies when you are running off the ball. Lure your marker in with a slow run, then suddenly sprint ahead into the clear to receive the pass. Vary the speed of your runs, with or without the ball, and you have added another skill that makes you a better player.

THE ONE-TWO (Fig. 18)

The one-two (wall pass, give and go) is extremely useful, a delight to see, and an artful but effective way to beat opposing players. It's particularly appropriate for indoor soccer, where the limited spaces invite quick, skillful one touch passing moves.

The technique requires a lot of practice from many different angles and distances. You dribble the ball directly at a defender to make him commit to a challenge. When he does that, the pass is knocked to your teammate, while you slip by the challenger in your stride and receive the return pass on the run. If correctly executed, the play leaves the opponent stranded facing the wrong way, as you continue the play on toward goal.

The name "one-two" describes the suddenness with which the one touch passes are made. The pass is knocked off "one", and comes back instantly first time "two". The timing that commits the defender to challenge, freezes him for an instant facing the wrong way. He can't turn quick enough to stay with his man, and the play goes by him.

The one-two should be practiced until it becomes second nature, because it can keep opponents off balance and nervous in their defensive efforts. The suddenness with which it can be used makes it a constant threat to set up a shot near goal.

In order to defend against the one-two, defenders find themselves giving the attackers more room to play, to avoid being caught slow in the turn. That's good news for attackers, so they should give the one-two lots of practice time.

THE ONE-TWO (Fig. 18)

Upper Center

(a) White #1 dribbles directly at Black #1 to make him commit to a challenge.
(b) Black #1 closes down to challenge White #1.
(c) White #1 passes to White #2, and runs on to receive a first time return pass and shoots on goal.

Lower Left

(a) White #2 supports White #1 by moving toward him.
(b) White #1 plays a pass to White #2 and runs to receive the first time return pass.

Lower Right

(a) White #2 moves to support White #1 and receives the pass.
(b) White #1 makes a run that frees him for the first time return pass.

Moving The Ball Forward With One-Two Passes. (Fig. 19)

White #1 uses a series of one-two passes with his teammates to move up the floor and create a shot on goal.

White players #2, #3, and #4 show themselves as target men and move toward the ball carrier, screening off their markers, to play one-two passes with White #1 and advance the ball toward the goal. One-two passes played forward and knocked back are an excellent way to move the ball upfield. They are usually easier and safer to play than through passes.

Fig. 18

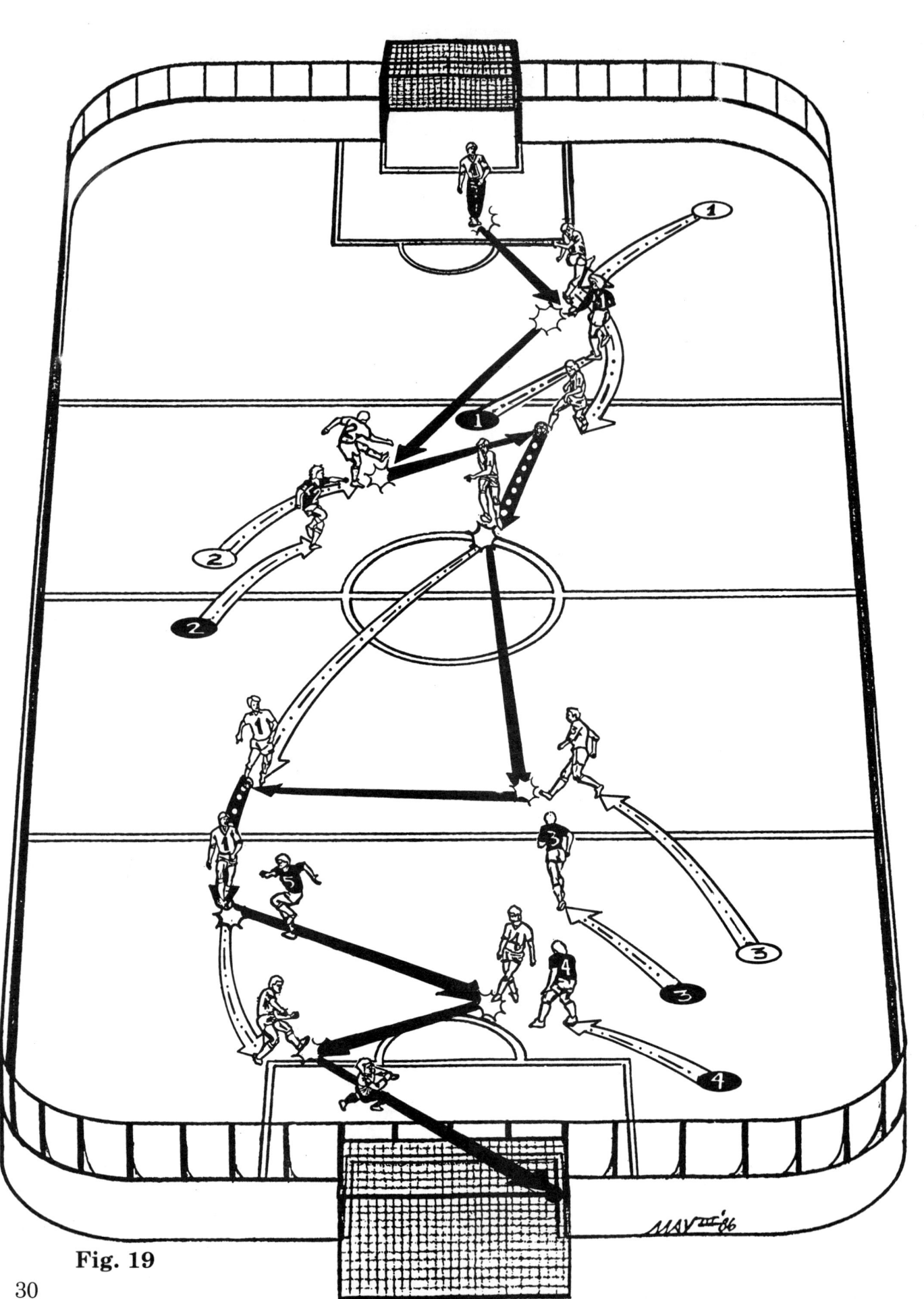

Fig. 19

CREATE TWO ON ONE (Commit the defender) (Fig. 20)

Attack defenders with the ball. Create two on one situations. If I'm in the clear with the ball at my feet, I should look for a teammate with a defender marking him. I dribble the ball right at the defender. My teammate moves away to the side. If his marker goes with him, I keep the ball and run on. If his marker stays to challenge me, I pass to my teammate. I then keep moving for a return pass.

Teamwork is required. Your teammate has to move at the right time to give you the option of keeping the ball or passing it. This is **support** play.

If you stand still your opponent can mark you with ease. Any pass directed toward you will be difficult to complete.

There may be times when you purposely stand still. You may pick a spot near the goal and remain there while some furious action takes place. Sometimes this action will pull your marker away from you leaving you open for a quick pass and shot. Experience and intuition will tell you when this might work. Sometimes you might stand still to set a pick for the ball carrier, or to screen off the goal keeper. There are exceptions for special tactics. In general you can't go wrong remembering that movement off the ball is the life blood of a soccer team's attack.

Because of the restricted space indoors, passing opportunities are fleeting. They come and go in a second or two. For this reason, you must read the game as it happens, so that you can time your movement to give the passer the best possible chance to get the ball to you.

Creating Two on One Situations (Fig. 20 "A")

(a) White #1 dribbles around Black #1.
(b) He then dribbles at Black #2.
(c) White #2 moves away.
(d) Black #2 stays to challenge for the ball, White #1 plays a one-two with White #2 and scores.

Creating Two on One Situations (Fig. 20 "B")

(a) White #1 dribbles around Black #1.
(b) White #1 dribbles **at** Black #2.
(c) White #2 moves away.
(d) Black #2 follows White #2.
(e) White #1 keeps the ball and shoots.

Creating two on one, and playing one-two passes are perhaps the two most important attacking moves in all of soccer play. They are relatively easy to learn, being a product of thought and vision mostly. No soccer player is complete without a full understanding of these two moves.

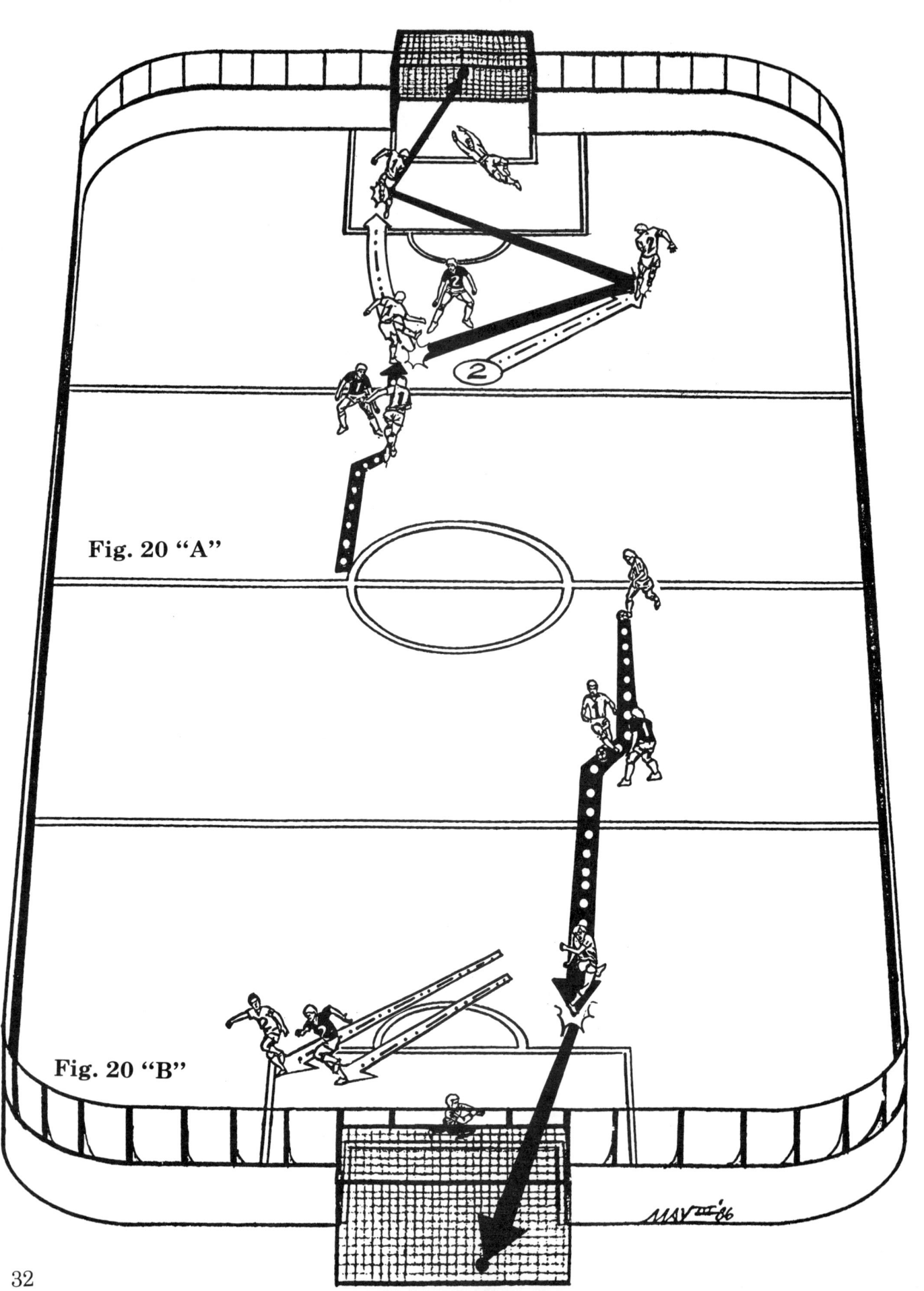

Fig. 20 "A"

Fig. 20 "B"

THE BACK-HEEL PASS

Imagine a pass that instantly reverses the direction of play, needs no preparation, and is virtually impossible to anticipate or prevent. That's the back-heel. It's not good for a long pass, and it's not used too often, but when it's called for, it's very effective.

When you are running with the ball and your progress is blocked, you often have a teammate trailing you to one side or the other. The back-heel pass can reach him easily and without warning. You play it in your running stride by taking a longer step that carries your foot past the ball. Just before your foot hits the floor, you strike the ball with a quick backward stab of your heel, sending it back and across your body to your oncoming teammate. It's a sudden movement, and it leaves your opponents flat footed. You have to glance out of the corner of your eye to make sure where your teammate is. You should never play the back-heel pass blindly, as inexperienced players are often seen to do. It's as likely to go to an opponent as to one of your players if you do. You must practice looking to the side and backward without turning your head so far that it tips your intentions to the opponents. When you are looking down at the ball, you don't have to turn your head very far to see behind you.

THE BACK-HEEL PASS (Fig. 21)

(a) Attacker #1 makes a run with the ball.
(b) He is held up by defenders #1 and #2
(c) He plays a back-heel pass to attacker #2 who has made a supporting run from the back and to the side of attacker #1
(d) Attacker #2 drives the ball first time into the goal

Fig. 21

THE BOARDS: AN EXTRA MAN

By far one of the biggest differences between indoor and outdoor soccer is the boards.

The boards surrounding the playing area are in reality an extra man for the attacking team. You can play wall passes to yourself on any part of the court. These can be especially dangerous when played so the rebound comes to you or a teammate right in front of the goal.

It's a good idea during the warm-up period before the game to check out the way the ball rebounds from different parts of the boards, so that in the game you will know what to expect. You will get an idea how hard to hit the ball when you play it off the wall, and how to time it. Most boards don't give the ball back to you in as lively a way as a player would. Also practice rebounding the ball from the rounded corner areas, so you get the right angle of rebound that you are after.

Playing The Ball Off The Boards (Fig. 22)

    1. White #1 dribbles in and plays a rebound pass near the corner of the goal, then plays the rebound into goal.

    2. White #1 beats his defender by playing a wall pass to himself.

3. White #1 beats his man by playing a wall pass to White #2, and then runs on to receive a return pass.

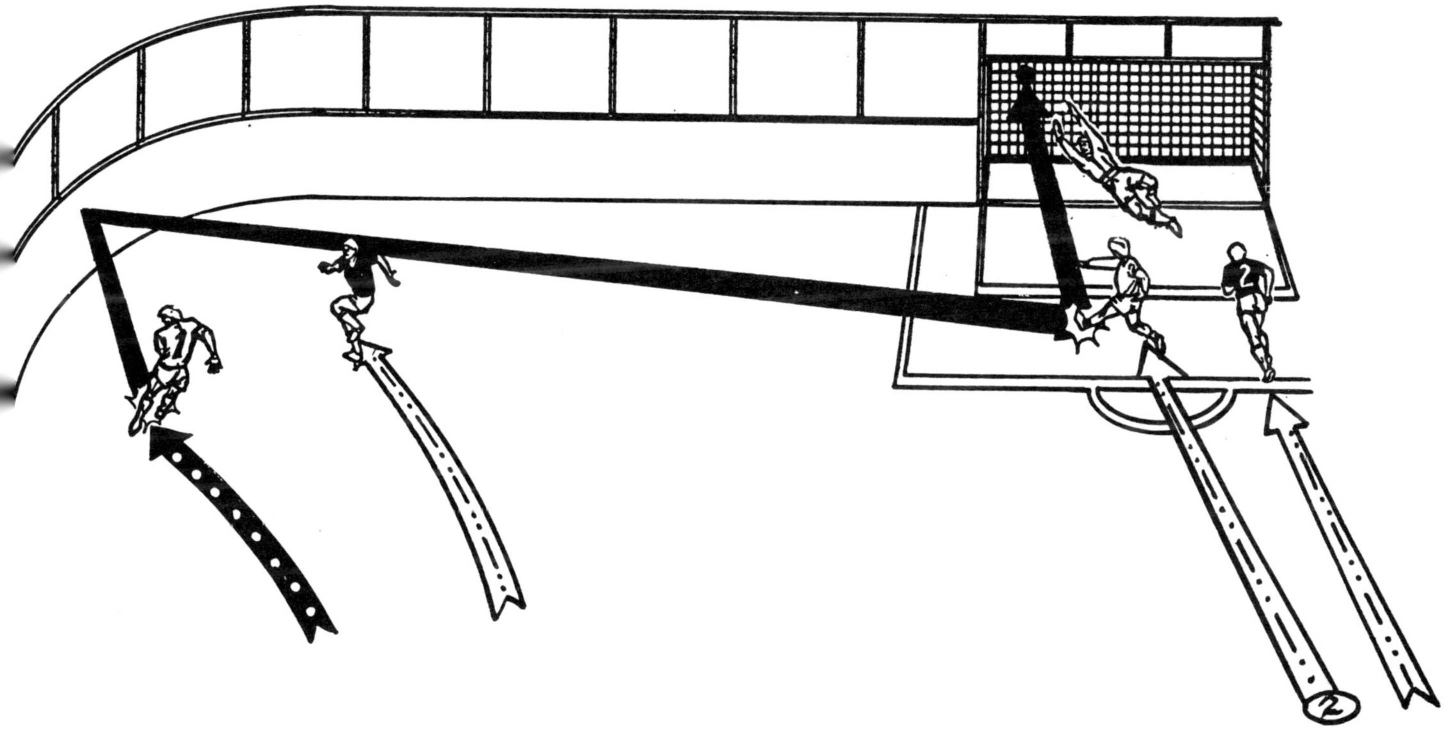

4. White #1 plays a wall pass that rebounds in front of goal. White #2 runs on to the rebound and shoots for goal.

Playing The Ball Off The Boards (Fig. 23) Top, next page

    (a) White #1 draws the goal keeper to the right corner by playing a wall pass to that spot.

    (b) White #2 runs on to the rebound, and shoots to the open left corner.

Fig. 23

Playing The Ball Off The Boards (Fig. 24)

(a) White #1 draws the keeper to the left corner by playing a ball to that spot. He runs on to his own rebound and shoots to the open right corner.

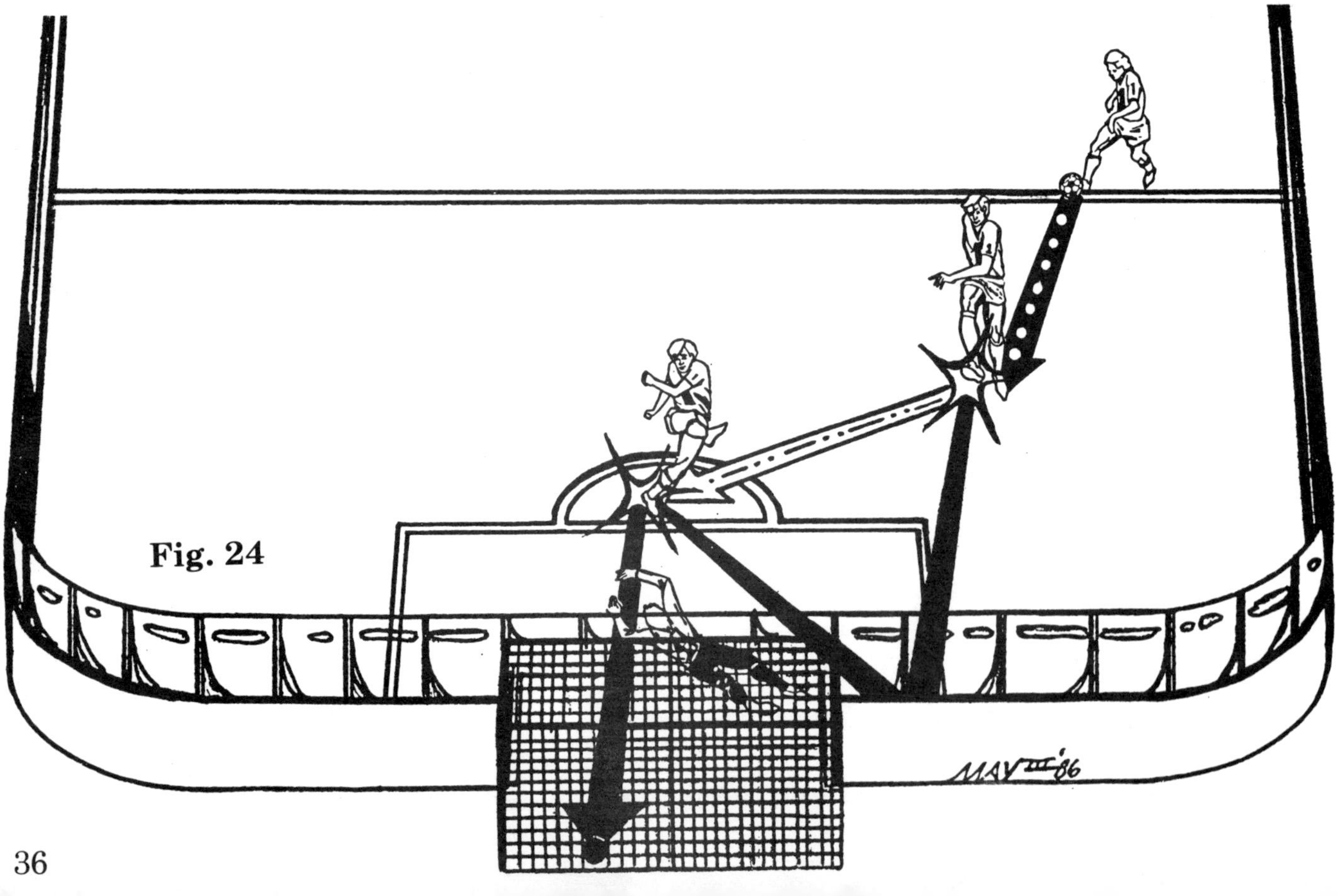

Fig. 24

Playing The Ball Off The Boards (Fig. 25)

(a) White #1 plays the ball up to the target man White #2.
(b) The target man lays it off first time to White #3.
(c) White #3 plays it to the boards for White #1 who shoots on goal.

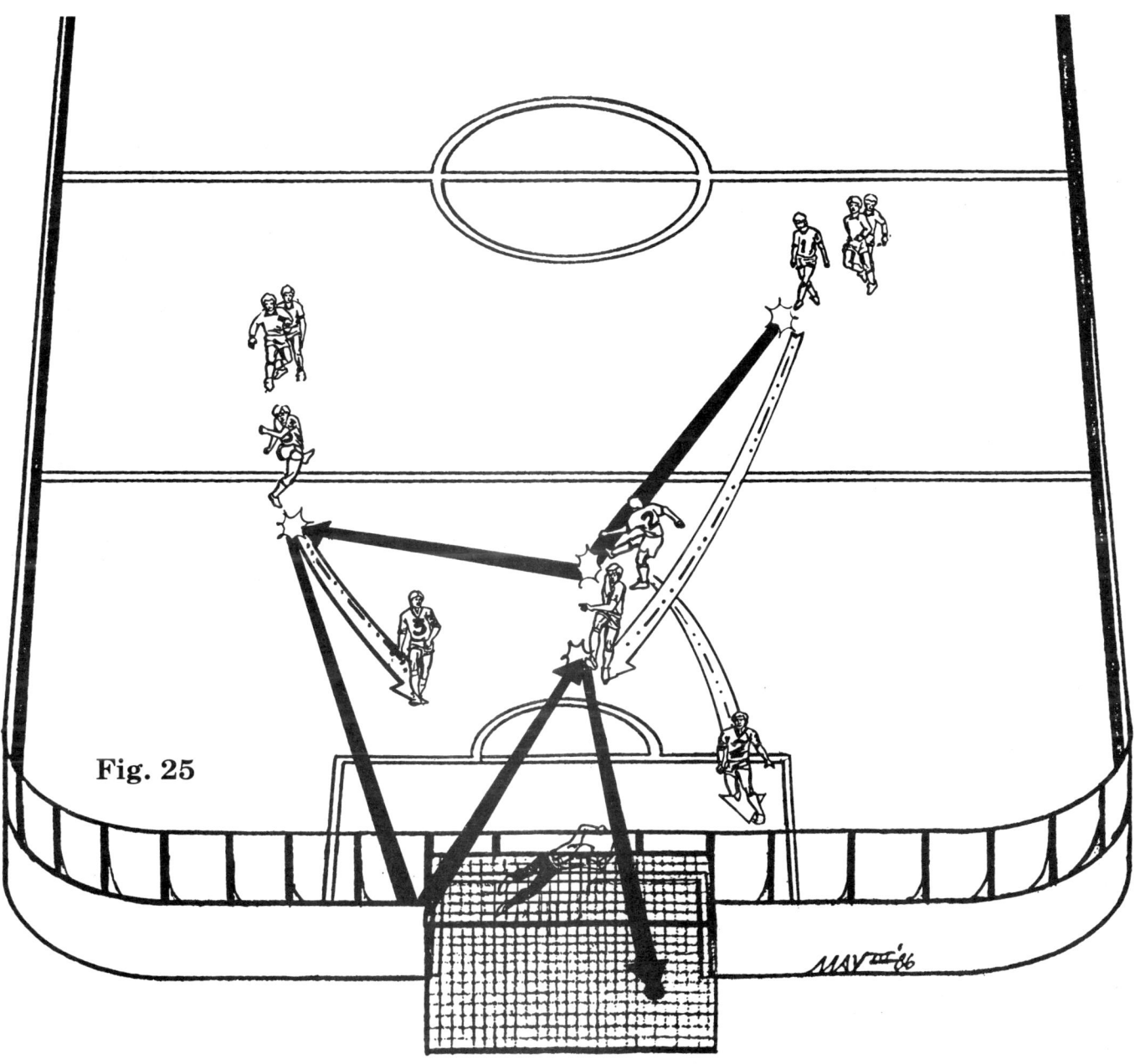

Fig. 25

The key to success is the **timing** of the runs by #1 and #3. This play and the other plays shown can all be used as drills by putting several players at each station and making the action continuous. Let all players use all the stations so that every one will become completely familiar with the play and recognize the situation when it comes up in a game. Work all the plays from **both** sides of the court.

Skillful use of the boards requires a lot of practice. It's like playing a bank shot on a pool table. You have to get just the right angle on your rebound to have it come back to you or another player at the right place and speed to be useful.

Practice whenever you can on a soccer court or any other place that has a rebound wall. When you can accurately pass the ball to yourself off a rebound from the boards around the goal, you have created an effective scoring tool. It looks simple, but it isn't. It takes a lot of practice to explore all the possible angles around the goal, and to **train your mind** to respond to the opportunities that come up with great speed around the goal. It's fun and adds a lot of deception to the attacking team.

Attacking play often becomes: pass the ball quickly out of defense; make crossing runs up front to advance the ball forward; and then use your skills with rebounds around the goal to finish off your attacks with shots on goal.

One thought to remember about your training: You'll be good at whatever you practice the most. In indoor soccer, playing the ball off the boards is a vital skill, so practice it whenever you can. It's hard to get practice time at a regular indoor court, so find a rebound wall. Mark a goal on it with tape 6½' high by 12' wide. If that wouldn't be allowed, mark off just the width with small patches of tape near gound level.

Play balls near to the corners at different angles, and then play the rebounds first time into the goal. With a friend you can play angles to each other for shots on the goal. If another friend is with you, put him in goal and try to score against him off rebounds.

Accuracy and **touch** are important in this practice. The balls have to rebound at the right angle and speed. It's much easier to play rebounds into goal **if the ball is kept on the floor.**

If the defenders and goal keepers say the ricochet off the boards is the hardest ball to defend against, then it's obviously worth a lot of practice time to perfect it.

Some of the illustrated plays shown in the book will suggest various rebound plays you can pratice. Make up your own as well.

From the Pros: **Mike Dowler:** Goal keeper for the **Tacoma Stars** of the **MISL**.

Question: "What's the most difficult part of the game for you?"

Answer: "Obviously the biggest thing has got to be the boards. Outdoors if the ball is going wide of the goal, it's going into the crowd, and it's going to be a goal kick."

"Indoors the boards keep that ball in play unless it's a very high shot. Just because the ball has whistled past the post, it doesn't mean you can relax. You must be alert and ready for the rebound. Some players will deliberately shoot wide trying to draw the keeper into a dive and hopefully hit the rebound into an empty net. So these are all things you must be aware of, and the ball knocked around the boards or around the glass. It sticks to the glass, bouncing each time, and you have to concentrate an awful lot to be able to catch the ball at the end of all that. I think thats the biggest single difference."

THE TARGET MAN OR POINT MAN

One way to create space in a lengthwise direction is to send a player forward to station himself in front of the opponent's goal. By doing this he will take a defender with him, thereby removing one opponent from the immediate area of play. He can also act as a target to play the ball up to, creating dangerous scoring chances right in front of goal. He posts up like a center in basketball.

He can play wall passes with his teammates; he can deflect shots past the goal keeper; he can turn with the ball himself and shoot; and he can retrieve loose balls and knock them back to start a new attack or for first time shots by other attackers.

The Target Man (Fig. 26)
    (a) White #1 passes up to the target man White #2.
    (b) White #2 holds off his defender, and passes to White #3 coming through.
    (c) White #3 shoots on goal.

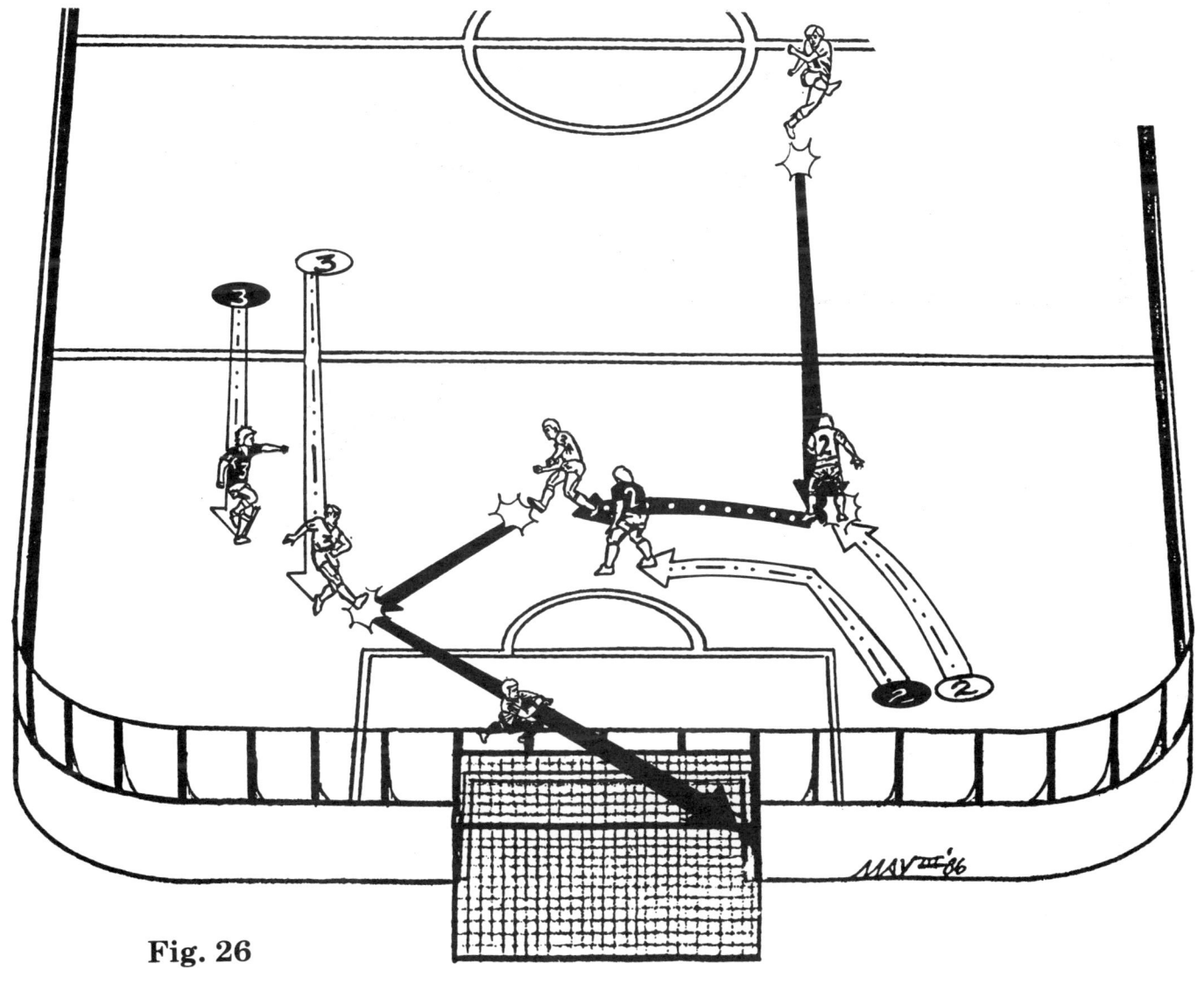

Fig. 26

The Target Man (Fig. 27)
    (a) White #1 plays a wall pass to the Target man White #2, and runs on for the return pass, and shoots for goal.
    (b) The defenders are beaten by the **speed** and **timing** of the runs and passes.

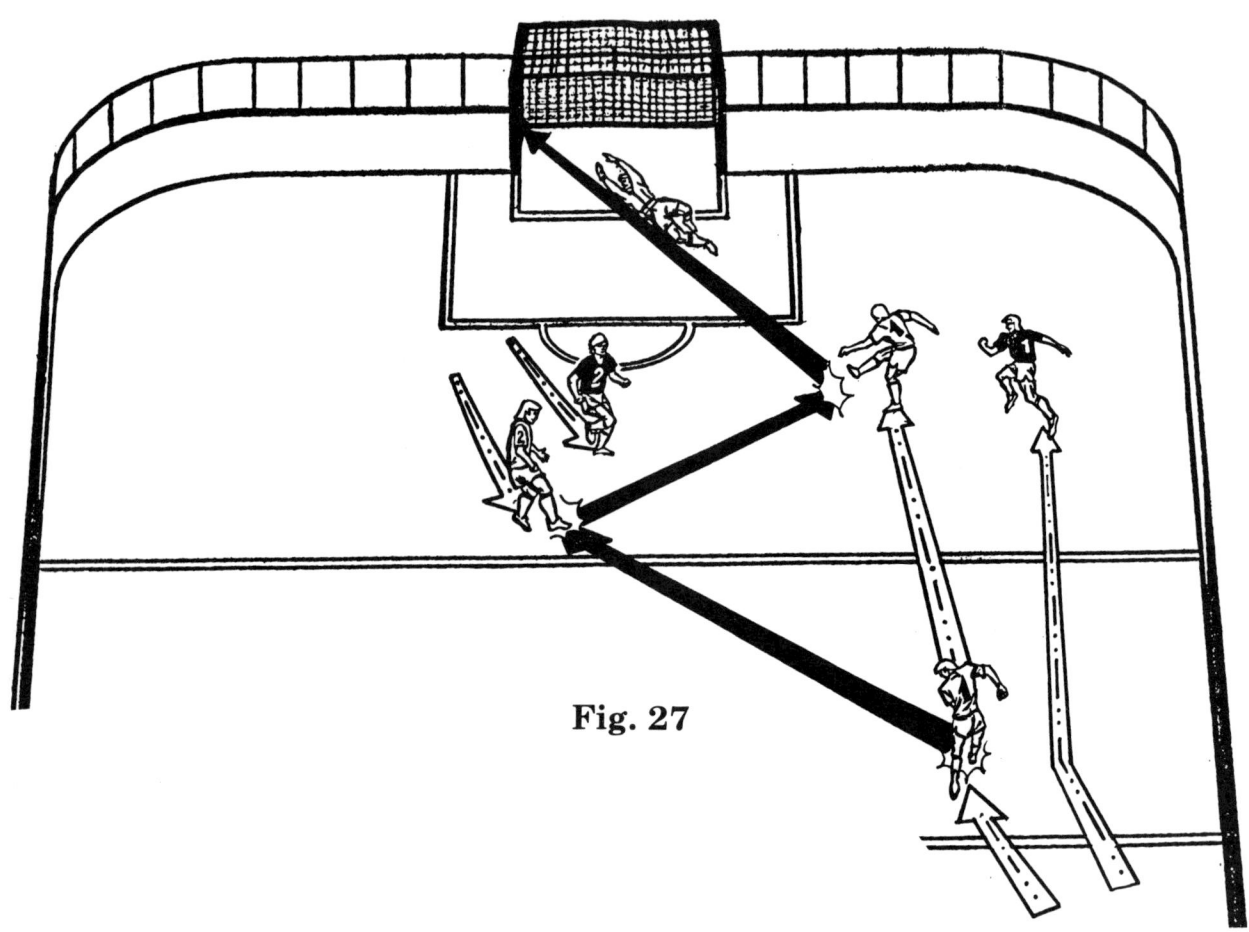

Fig. 27

Fig. 28

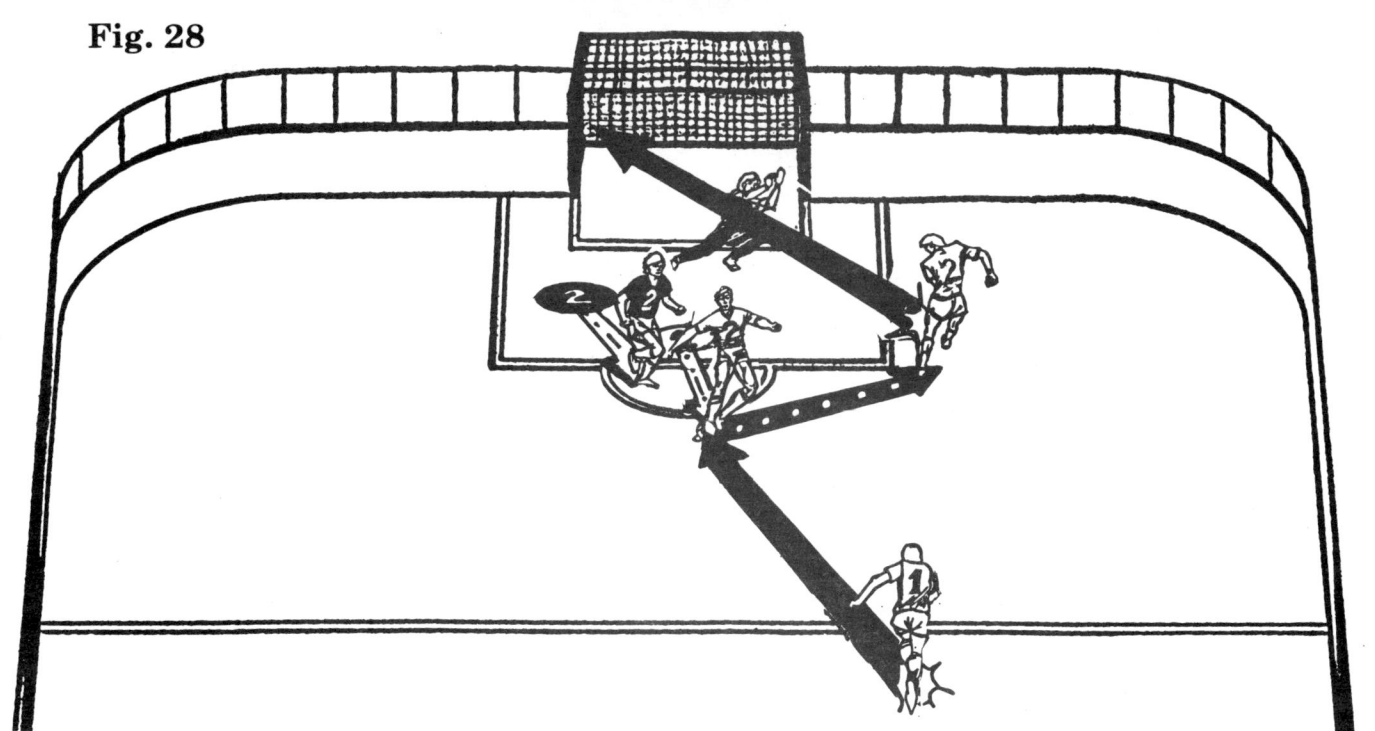

The Target Man (Fig. 28)
    (a) White #1 plays a pass up to the target man White #2.
    (b) The target man moves onto the ball screening off his defender.
    (c) He deflects the ball past his defender, and runs on to it and shoots.

Fig. 29

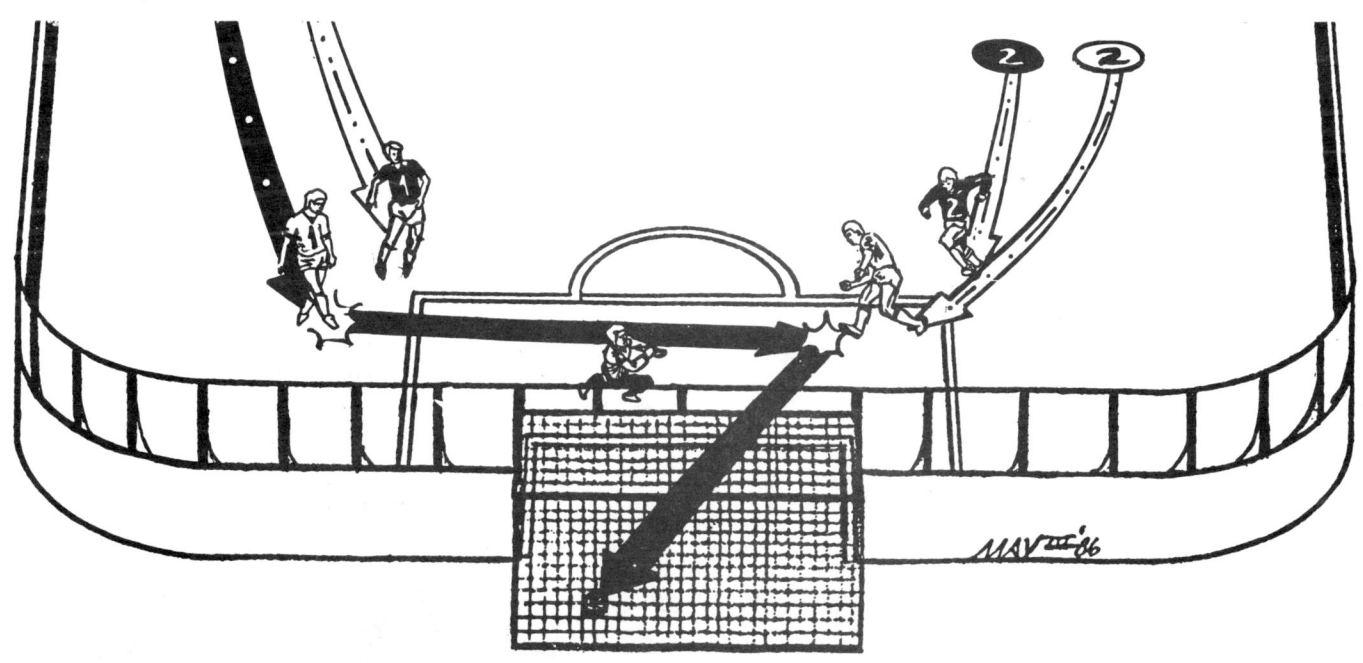

The Target Man (Fig. 29)
    (a) White #1 dribbles the ball down the side line, and crosses a pass in front of goal.
    (b) The target man White #2 beats his man to the ball and deflects it into goal.

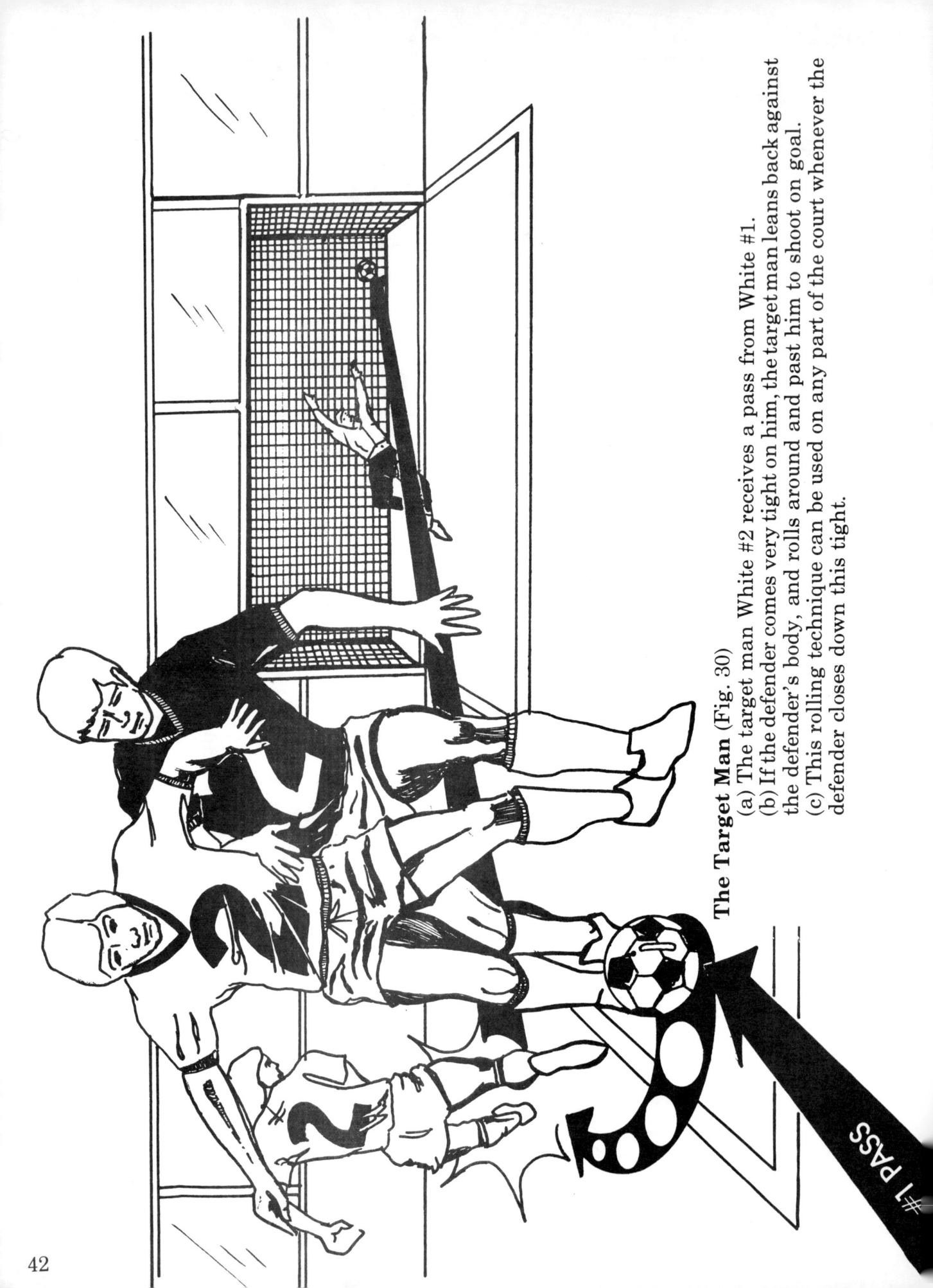

The Target Man (Fig. 30)
(a) The target man White #2 receives a pass from White #1.
(b) If the defender comes very tight on him, the target man leans back against the defender's body, and rolls around and past him to shoot on goal.
(c) This rolling technique can be used on any part of the court whenever the defender closes down this tight.

From the **Chicago Sting** of the (MISL), head coach **Willy Roy;** Forward **Karl Heintz Granitza;** and Defender **Neil Roberts** discuss the target man's play.

Question to Willy Roy: "What attacking strategies do you try to acquire as a team?"

Answer: "I think the important thing is you have to formulate your attack according to the players that you have. If you have two quick forwards, then you can hit a lot longer passes. We have a different style with Karl Heintz Granitza. We have more of a **control game.** We try to play the ball up to him, and then run off of him, either defenders or midfielders running off of him. So it depends on the type of players that you have, how you formulate your offense."

Question: "Which qualities are most desirable in an indoor soccer player?"

Answer: "Well obviously you want a player who is a winner to begin with. That's number one—the desire to win. The other thing of course from the skill factor, I think when you build a team you have to build a team with the right chemistry. You like to have a good **point man** up in the forward line who can hold the ball and relieve the defense a little bit when they pass the ball up. You need some quick defenders that can run out of the back and have shooting ability, that they can score goals."

"Then you need midfielders that have an unbelievable pace running up and down chasing, playing offense and defense. So if you are looking to describe a good indoor soccer player, I think he's got to be **intelligent,** he's got to be **quick,** he's got to be **durable,** and he's got to be **aggressive.**"

Question to Karl Heintz Granitza: "As an attacker, what's the hardest part of the game for you?"

Answer: "I think the most important part is your **holding** the ball for your teammates. You have to give a lift and breathing room for the defensing players on your team, that's indoors and also outdoors. When you **control** the ball in the forward line, you're creating opportunity. And that's the second point, creating opportunity, and working very, very hard to get the ball and try to find the ball all the time. That's the hardest part."

Question to Neil Roberts: "In your training sessions, what skills and tactics do you work on the most as a defender?"

Answer: "We practice a lot of intra squad scrimmages where you're just getting to know the other players and you look to play the ball deep from your own defensive zone to the front men and then **supporting** them. That's the most important thing. We've got a player like Karl Heintz Granitza who can **hold** the ball up for you, and wait for the other people such as myself to support them. This sort of practice is just to get an understanding of the others' play. It's very important to have a good player such as we have, and many teams around the league have, where that front man has very good skills with his **back to the goal,** and he can control the ball and wait for support from the midfielders and defenders."

Many amateur teams neglect this target man method of attack. They continually try for through passes in crowded areas with little chance of success.

In fact, all players should practice as target men on all parts of the court. It's the easiest and the safest way to move the ball forward. You are playing facing your own goal. By timing your move correctly, you show yourself to the man on the ball and move toward him. He plays the ball to you, and moves off to receive the return pass.

The reason this maneuver works so well is because the target man automatically shields the ball by moving toward it, and the man receiving the return pass is facing the ball as it comes back to him. Often when the target man moves toward the ball, his defender moves with him creating space in which to play the return pass.

A series of two or three wall passes in this manner often creates a shot on goal.

SHIELDING THE BALL (Fig. 30)

Shielding the ball is your most valuable skill as a target or point man. Without it you can't hold the ball long enough for your teammates to make runs.

You shield the ball by keeping yourself between your defender and the ball so that he can't get the ball without fouling you. If you simply turn your back to your defender, you can't keep him far enough away. He can stick his foot in between your legs and knock the ball free. You have to fend him off with your shoulder, while your opposite foot controls the ball. If you are fending him off with your left shoulder, your right foot controls the ball and vice versa. You keep turned sideways to your defender.

The hard part is to keep this sideways position as your opponent struggles to outmaneuver you and get at the ball. You have to keep your opponents movement and the ball in sight at the same time. Not easy, but a lot of practice helps.

As you lean into your defender, you can tell by feel what he is doing to a certain extent. Your success depends on your sense of balance and your ability to shift your weight in a way that will keep your opponent from knocking you off the ball.

With an opponent, start by shielding the ball in one place. When you can do this, shield it as you move in different directions. Then shield the ball as you back into your opponent and try to roll past him on either side. Keep at this kind of practice until shielding the ball becomes instinctive. Then you can handle yourself with confidence in the close quarters of indoor soccer.

Sometimes this technique requires watching the ball with your eyes and playing the man by "feel". Sometimes it's the other way around, watching the man and playing the ball by feel. Ideally it's nice to be able to see both the man and the ball at the same time. Your peripheral vision will help you. By training your eyes this way, you establish your balance and poise in tight situations and build your confidence as a ball handler.

CONTROL

Control describes how a player receives a pass. When receiving the ball you have to reduce it's speed or stop it, or change it's direction so you can play it again or dribble it. That's control, and **practice** makes it work.

Control, as applied to soccer, can have other meanings. It can apply to a team's general demeanor. They run under control, they react to the situations of the game without panic. Even at the most frantic moments, they know what's going on. At tremendous speeds they can stop, turn, jump, etc., and never give the impression they have abandoned authority over themselves.

Professionals play faster than amateurs because their fitness is higher, their **control** is quicker, and they play or train everyday. Daily training tunes their senses, so they react without thinking too much about what they are doing. Thinking takes time. Training cuts down thinking time. The indoor game is mostly reaction and reflexes when you're in close quarters.

The faster you play, the more skill is required. Inexperienced players often try to play faster than their abilities allow.

It's better to work hard at several control and dribbling moves that allow you to play slower, and within yourself but still avoid the onrushing players who fly in for tackles.

Beginning players should spend time learning to receive and **trap** the ball from different angles. Learn how to shield it from opponents, and perfect the **push pass** made with the inside of the foot. This pass is far easier to learn than the instep kick, and it's more accurate. It's plenty good enough for most of the passes that will be made indoors, and it's the pass most used by professionals.

Professionals don't do things the hard way. They do things the easiest possible way. The game is hard enough to play without inventing new and more difficult ways to get the ball from point A to point B.

Soccer is a kicking game, so obviously you should spend a great deal of your time on **kicking** and **trapping**, skills. Trapping is relatively easy if you remember **to let the ball hit you,** rather than vice-versa. Just present the part of you at which the ball is coming and **let the ball hit it.** For balls coming along the floor, this means the inside, the outside, or the sole of the foot. For balls coming in about waist high, it would be the inside, outside, or front of the thigh. Infrequently you will use the chest trap.

One rule is unalterable. You must have no tension whatsoever in the part of you doing the trapping. Your instincts tell you to hit the ball. Don't. Just **let the ball hit you**. Once you can do this, most of your trapping difficulties are over. From then on, you will be amazed at how easy it is to take the pace off the ball, and lay it right where you want it, so you can make the next play, either pass or dribble.

The **push pass** is another quite simple move. The hips are turned out, and the ball is struck on the firm part of the inside of the ankle.

Learn these two techniques, and you are on your way to much greater enjoyment and accomplishment than you may have thought possible. **Seek** out players who can teach you these two things. They are indispensable and really quite easy to learn. Remember to step forward as you strike the ball. This gets your weight into the kick, and gives greater **control**, accuracy, and distance.

When receiving the ball, **allow it to hit the trapping surface,** and allow the trapping surface to "give" and **absorb** the speed of the moving ball. With study, practice, and experience, you will learn how to stop the ball dead, or change the ball's direction as you trap it, all in one movement.

Ball skills become more difficult when you have to reach for the ball. **Control** your movement so you are in position to receive the ball without reaching for it. Control applies to trapping the ball, passing the ball, and running both with and without the ball. It also means managing your emotions and concentration so your body can perform at its best.

If you can learn to hook the ball with the inside of either foot, and brush it sideways with the outside of either foot, you have four dribbling moves that will help you get past opposing players. Work diligently at these things, and you'll start to gain control over your game, and that's what it's all about.

Amateurs should practice and play as much as possible to improve their reaction time and to make their **technique** more automatic.

From the Pro's: **Greg Blasingame,** talented young player of the **Tacoma Stars** of the **MISL**.

Question: "What did you find was the hardest transition to make, coming into the indoor game and into the professional game?"

Answer: "I think there's a couple of aspects. The quickness is just immense in indoor. There are a lot of **reactionary** situations. I also think the use of the boards is another key role to learn before you can perfect the indoor game."

Question: "What would you say young amateur players, coming up in the indoor game, should work on?"

Answer: "I think they should first of all try to have the endurance. If you don't have the stamina to go out there and play a full game, your performance is going to go down, because you're too tired to do what you want to do. Secondly, I think it's important to get the feel of the ball. Practice juggling and other **ball control** things on your own time. You don't need anybody around you for that type of thing. That will improve your passing and dribbling skills. And I think the important thing to do is to try to get into as many indoor games as you can."

If you sense the difference between **applying** force to the ball when you kick it, and **absorbing** force from the ball when you trap it, your **control** of the ball will increase.

Although the playing area is limited, there is **space** available. You have to find it or create it, and then use it.

Space may be conceded to you by the defending team through their positioning. In that case it's a simple matter to play the ball up into this space. Most times you will have to make your own space by the players without the ball running constantly into new positions; thereby leaving space behind them for their teammates to move into; and opening angles for passes.

In order to maintain possession and to move the ball forward, **first time** passing often has to be used. Players should constantly work on their passing and receiving skills, because in the indoor game, play is greatly accelerated and the ball moves from end to end at high speed.

THE KICK-OFF

The kick-off is usually taken by a short tap into the opponent's half, and then the ball is knocked back to one of the defenders. The attacking players should spread out, using the full width of the court, and pass the ball among themselves in their own half until some of the defending players have been drawn toward them. When the defending players move in to attempt to capture the ball, they will open up some space behind them for the attackers to pass and move into.

When attacking, remember you always have an extra man in your goal keeper, so in theory you should never give the ball away in your own half.

Typical Kick-off Movement (Fig. 31)
    (a) White #1 taps the ball across the midfield line to White #2. Who knocks it back to White #3.
    (b) Black #1 and #3 follow the ball leaving space behind them for the attackers to move into.
    (c) The attackers spread the play lengthwise and widthwise to create space into which to play the ball. White #3, to White #4, to White #1, to White #2.
    (d) White #1 and White #5 support the play. White #5 shoots for goal.

Another possible kick-off move (Fig. 32)
    (a) White #1 taps to White #2.
    (b) White #2 dribbles to make room for himself, and then passes to White #1 who has made a run.
    (c) White #1 turns and plays a ball off the wall to White #3, who has run in support of the play.

    (d) White #3 shoots for goal.

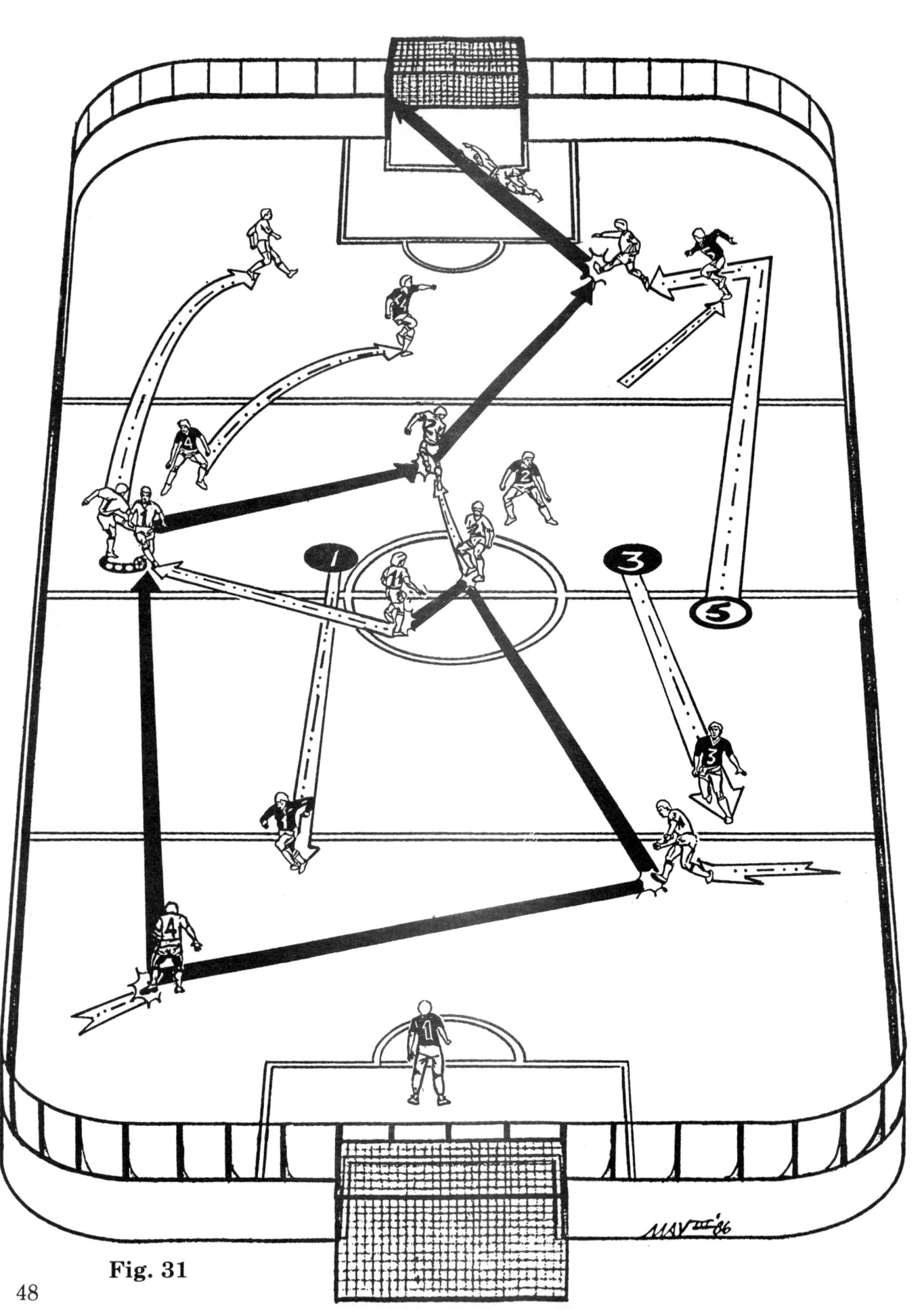

Fig. 31

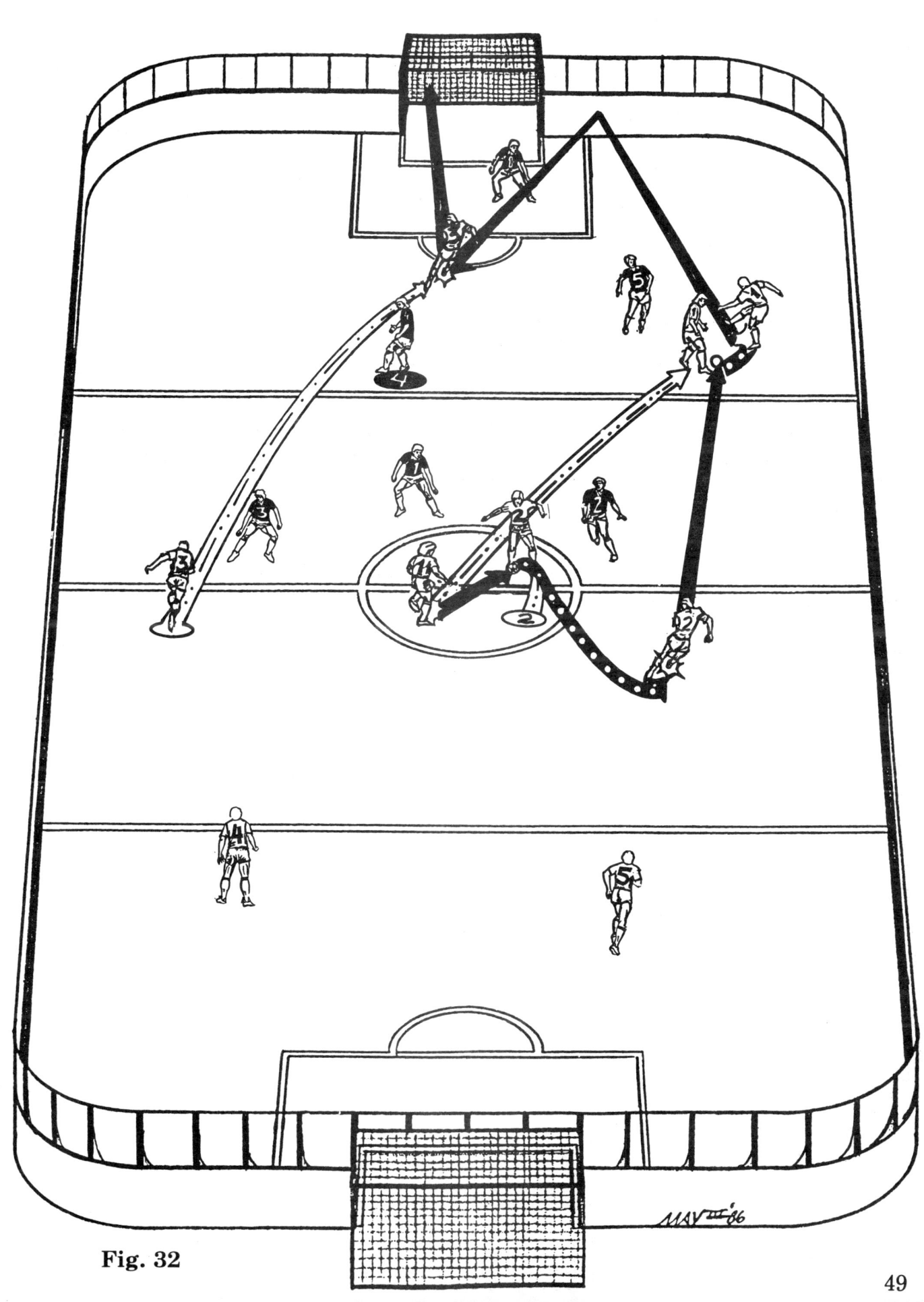

Fig. 32

Kick-off Play: Create 3 on 2 (Fig. 33)
>(a) White #1 taps the ball to White #2, and then runs on for the return pass, beating Black #1.
>(b) White #1 dribbles on and beats Black #4, and plays the ball off the boards for White #2 who shoots.
>(c) White #3 makes a supporting run to be ready to receive a pass from White #1 or #2, or to pounce on a muffed stop by the keeper, or a rebound off the boards.

Kick-off Move (Fig. 34)
>(a) White #1 taps the ball to White #2.
>(b) White #2 knocks it back to White #3.
>(c) White #3 plays it **first time** to White #4.
>(d) White #4 then plays it to White #2.
>(e) White #2 can try to score, or he might pass to White #1 or #4 who make supporting runs.

This is a very quick opening move. The first three passes are one touch passes for instant penetration on the goal. If the attackers are very aggressive in their runs, they can force errors from the defense right in front of goal. Even if the ball is lost, it's deep in the attacking zone, allowing the team who lost it lots of space in which to recover.

The professional teams are becoming much more direct and aggressive in attacking with various kick-off plays. It seems to be a more profitable way to go in the indoor game. It puts the defense under immediate pressure, and can often create instant scoring possibilities. It's always better to play the game in the opponents half instead of yours.

Fig. 33

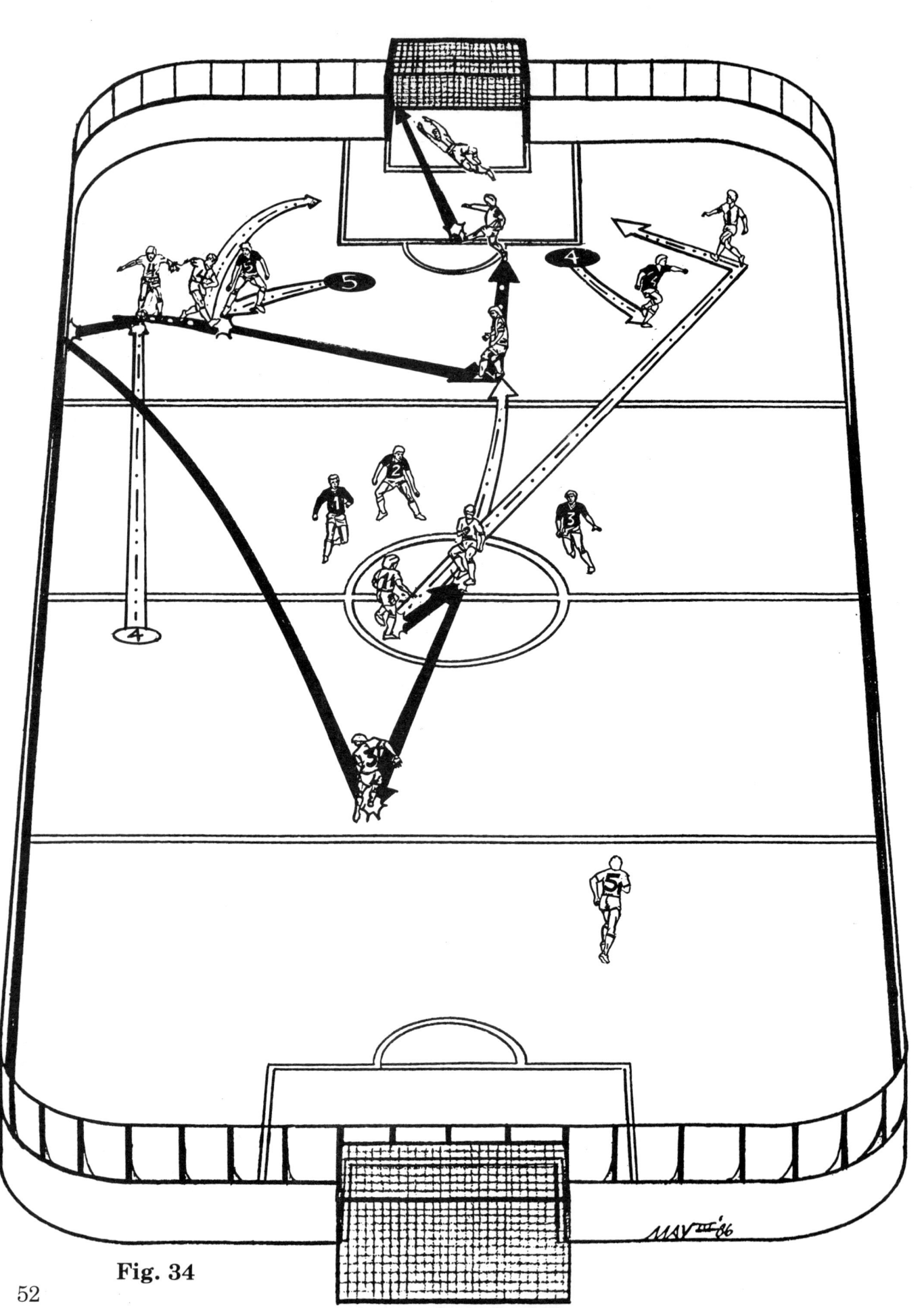

Fig. 34

SUPPORT PLAY IN ATTACK

Support the man on the ball. Support him by being available to him. You'll run and not receive the ball many times, but your movement **takes defending players out of the way** and makes **space.**

Your movement off the ball gives him the **option** to pass or keep the ball. As you move out of an area, you leave space behind. The man on the ball can use this space by dribbling into it or passing into it to another player running to receive the ball. Support should be instantaneous and constant. You can't play successfully without it.

The timing of the runs must be right in order for supporting play to be effective. If your teammate is making a run, you have to time your pass so that it arrives just ahead of him, so he can receive it in his stride. Don't worry too much that you'll play the ball too far ahead of him. Usually it's too far behind him, forcing him to stop and wait for it.

From the pro's: **Brian Quinn,** Midfielder for the **San Diego Sockers** of the **MISL.**

Question: "What about the importance of movement in creating space?"

Answer: "I think stressing to young kids when they are starting to play indoor soccer to realize if you don't have the ball, you have to think about the game."

"Create space for other people and listen to your coach, and do the drills where you are not involved. You open big holes in the defense for other players to go through and have shots on the target."

Doc Lawson: Defender, **Dallas Sidekicks** of the **MISL.**

Question: "Is there any particular way you like to move the ball out of your defensive end, so it's easy and safe?"

Answer: "Oh sure, we always try to spread our backs out wide enough so we can create an opening down the middle and possibly get the ball down the middle to one of our strikers. That's one way of getting out of the defense."

"Another way is we try to utilize our goal keeper if he's skillful enough, to bring the ball up and maybe chip passes. We try to spread them out again and pull players away from the middle and give the ball to the goal keeper and have him dribble into the red zone and then try to get it behind the defenders into the boards."

"We want to bring their players into our zone a little bit, so we can create space in the front for players to perhaps make runs. Sometimes we have our forwards making criss-cross runs to create openings. We'll drop back, feed the ball to the goal keeper, and immediately after the ball is fed back, the two front players make criss-cross runs to create openings for the ball to be thrown out to them."

"Sometimes it's better playing the ball to your defenders, and then we create space by having our midfielders move away so we can play the ball down along the boards to create another form of opening there for the forwards running into the pass."

The critical thing is that all members of the team enter into the business of support. It means you are willing to work for each other. One player who shirks his duty breaks down the continuity of play.

Peter Ward of the **Cleveland Force** of the **MISL** on teamwork.

"You want to work for your teammates, as they want to work for you. Every game's a hard game—and we look forward to every game. We take one game at a time and we want to get to the championship."

Support in attack means making yourself available to the man with the ball so that he has the option of one or more passing possibilities or of keeping the ball and running with it. The thing that makes support work is intelligent, well timed movement by all members of the team. The reward: You get the feeling of comradeship that comes with playing as a team.

Support Play (Fig. 35)

>(a) White #1 receives the ball from the keeper.
>(b) White #2 makes a run, taking his defender out of the ball carrier's path.
>(c) White #3 does the same thing.
>(d) White #1 attacks Black #4 by dribbling the ball at him.
>(e) White #4 moves away to receive a pass and shoot.
>(f) If Black #4 moves off to mark White #4, White #1 keeps the ball and shoots.

Creating Space By Running Off The Ball (Fig. 36)

>(a) By their movement, White #2 and #4 create space behind themselves. (indicated by shaded circles)
>(b) White #3 and #5 can move into this space to receive passes.
>(c) White #1 can play the ball to White #3 and #5.
>(d) Continuing this process enables the attacking team to maintain possession and penetrate the defenses of the opposing team.

Creating Space By Running Off The Ball (Fig. 37)

>(a) White #3 makes a run leaving space behind for White #2 to receive a pass and shoot.
>(b) The space created by White #3's run is shown by a shaded circle.

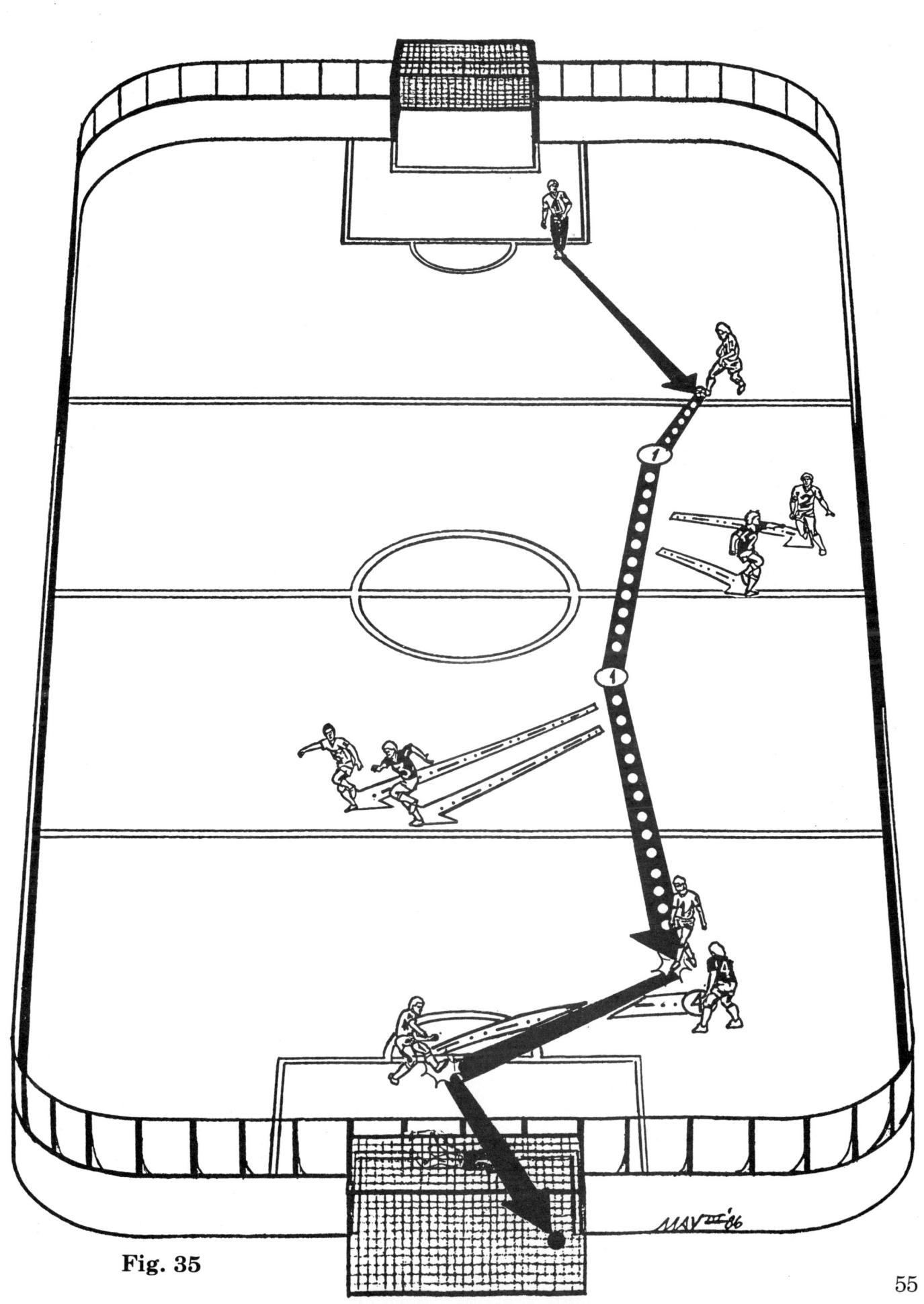

Fig. 35

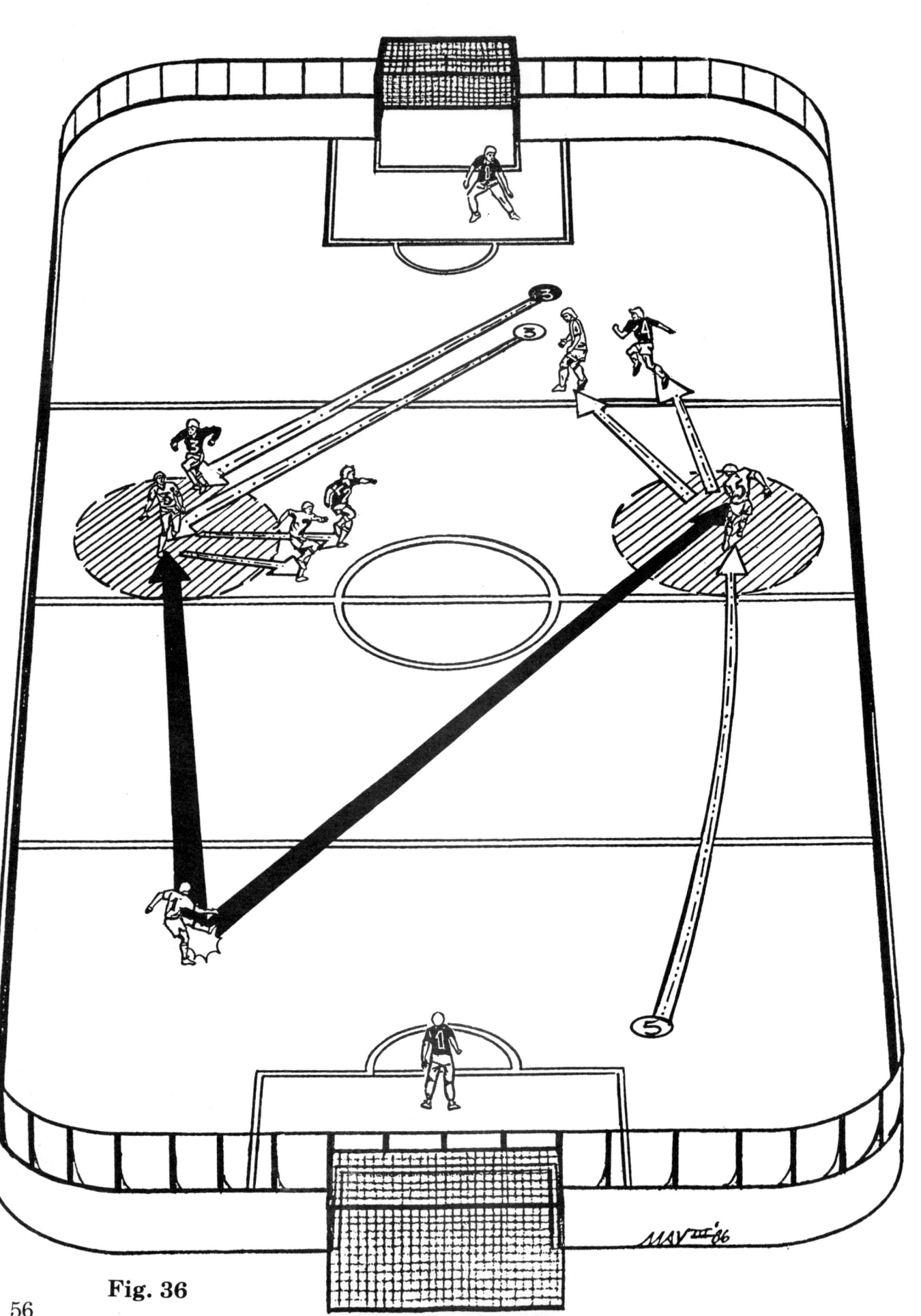

Fig. 36

Fig. 37

Making Attacking Runs (Fig. 38)

(a) By running a slanting pattern, White #2 can screen off his marker and receive the ball.

Making Attacking Runs (Fig. 39)

(a) By running a "hook" pattern, White #2 screens off his defender and can receive the ball in close quarters.
(b) White #2 can then play a return pass to White #1 for a shot.

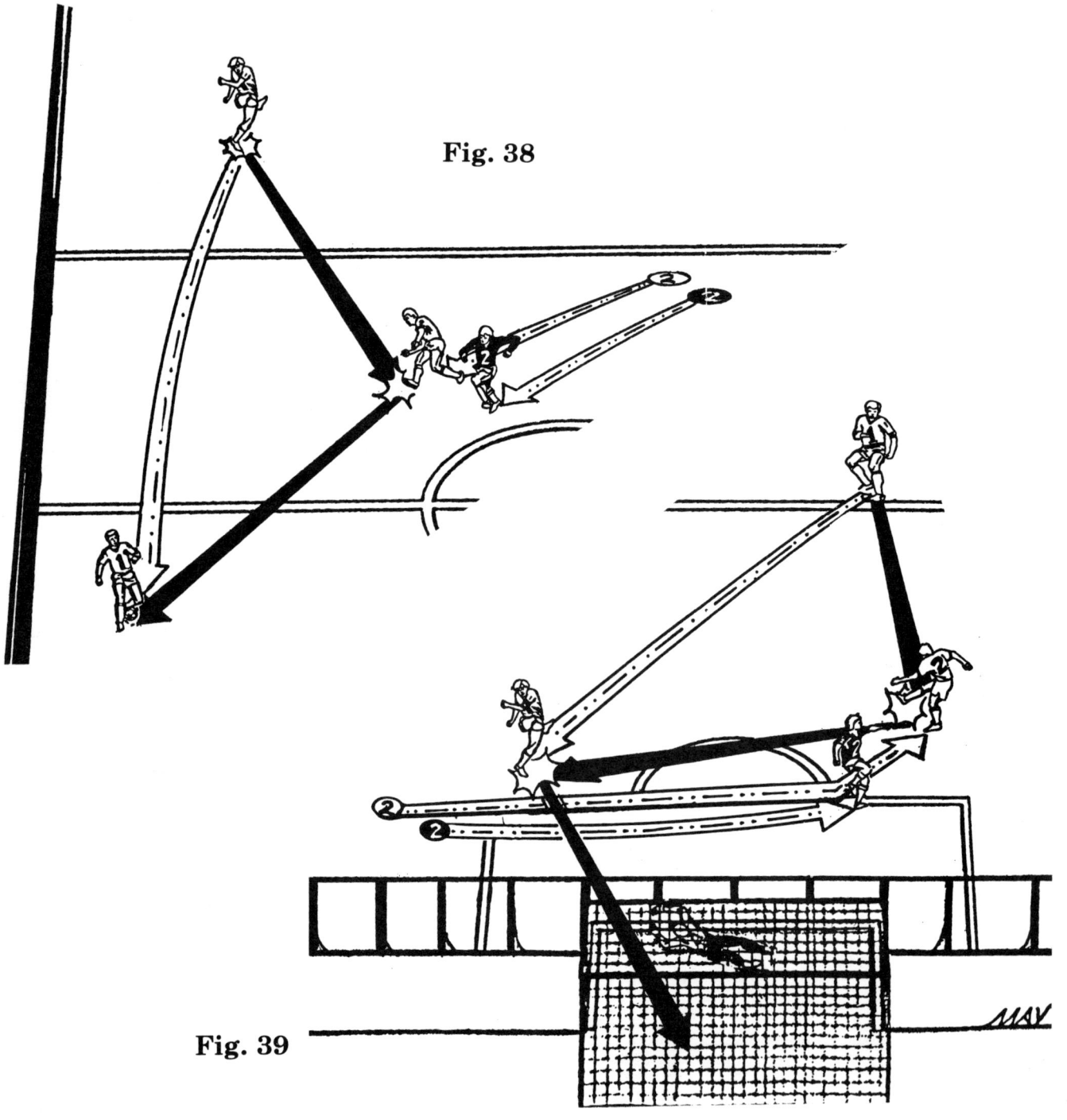

Fig. 38

Fig. 39

Forwards will be playing with their backs to the goal a lot of the time. They have to work hard to find the ball, and then lay it back to people making runs. Many amateur players neglect to play this easy ball back. There is a time to turn with the pass, and there is a time to play the ball back one-two. Forwards have to develop the vision and soccer sense to make the right choices. One move sets up the other. If you always do the same thing, you become predictable, and make it easier on your defender.

Defenders often err in this situation too. They pass the ball forward and then stay back. Frequently there is space to go forward into attacking areas for the return pass, and follow up with attacking moves. If back players do go forward, they should cover for each other to balance the shape of their attack, or a midfielder should rotate back to cover any space left by the back player's attacking move.

FOLLOW UP YOUR PLAY

When you take a shot on goal, follow up the ball in case it's mishandled by the keeper, or ricochets off the boards or another player, giving you another chance at it. The same applies when you play a pass. Follow the play to receive a return pass, or to close down on an opponent, if the pass is intercepted.

This way you continue to make things happen, and put constant pressure on the opposing team. Jean Willrich of the San Diego Sockers is a fine example of this kind of play. He has immense strength and energy, and always follows up his passes and shots, creating something out of nothing, where the average player would tend to make the shot or pass and then stop to see the results. Jean never waits. He's always on top of the ball, the eternal opportunist, making him a constant threat. When you follow up your pass or shot, you are **supporting** your own play.

MAKING SPACE FOR YOURSELF

You can make space for **yourself** by your **movement,** just as you can make space for someone else.

You move out of an area leaving space behind you, and then check back into this space to receive the ball. Correct **timing** by the runner and the passer is needed to make it work. The runner has to wait until the passer can see him, and then make his move quickly. The passer has to play the ball when the runner is in a position to beat his defender to it. It's a very useful maneuver, and hard to stop when it's **executed** properly. It's a good way to break down tight marking, and it's great fun to beat a defender with this kind of running.

Making Space For Yourself (Fig. 40)

    (a) White #2 makes a run **toward** White #1 who has the ball.
    (b) Black #2 is drawn in by the move.
    (c) White #2 suddenly checks back in to the space his run has created.
    (d) White #1 plays the ball into the path of White #2.
    (e) White #1 makes a supporting run to be available for a return pass.

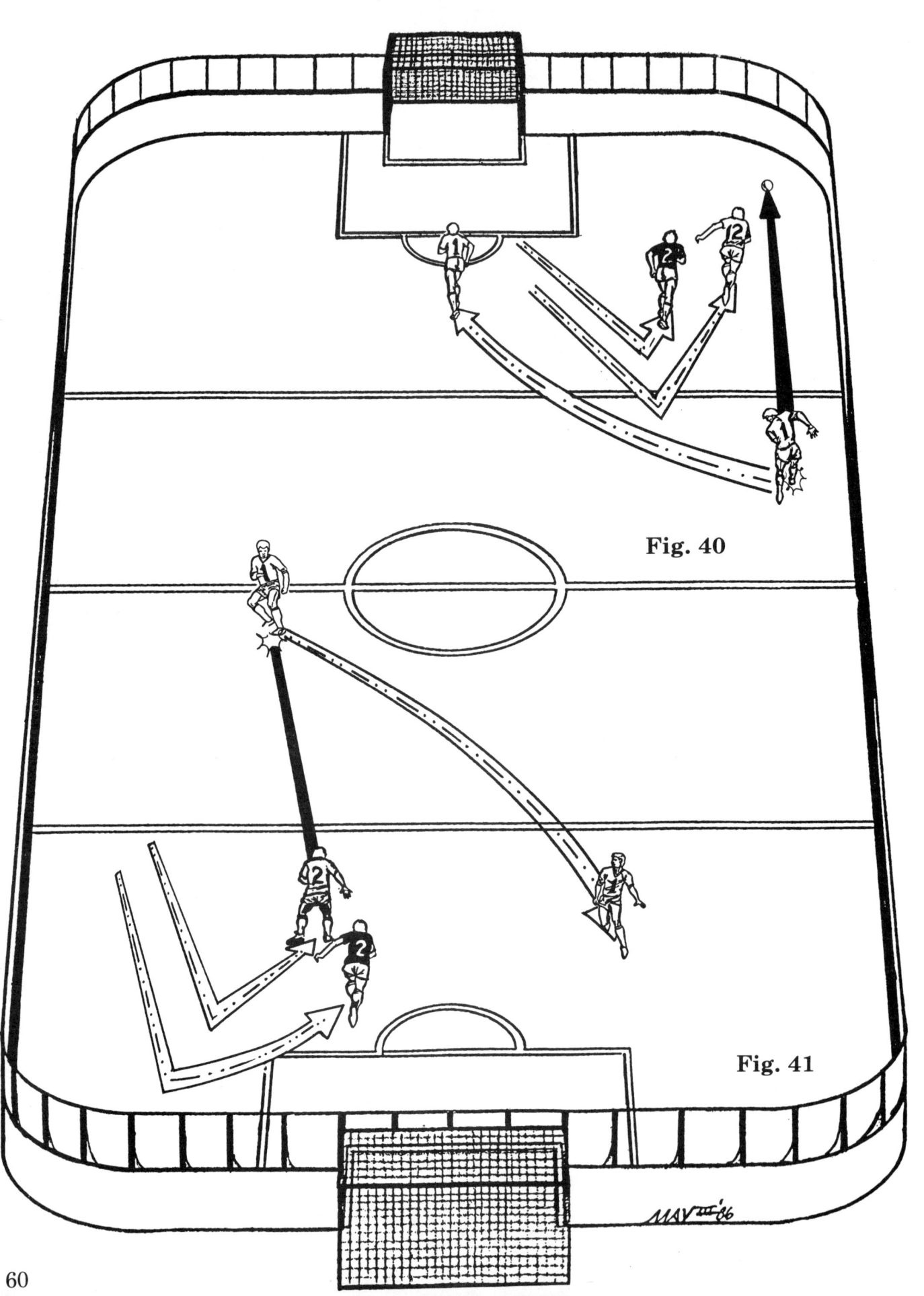

Fig. 40

Fig. 41

Making Space For Yourself (Fig. 41)

(a) White #2 makes a run **away** from White #1, taking with him Black #2.
(b) He suddenly checks back into the space his run has created.
(c) White #1 plays the pass to White #2, and then runs in support of the play for a possible return pass.

Mark Kerlin: Forward, **Baltimore Blast** of the **MISL**.

"If you get kids at a young age to just play, lets say one or two touch, they'll **have** to run off the ball. Otherwise they won't be able to play. They'll be giving up the ball all the time. If you get them to play two or three touches, they have to pass the ball and make a run to an open space so they can receive it back. That's how you get that type of play going."

THE BACK PASS

Frequently the ball is lost when a player attempts to dribble or pass the ball forward when there are too many opponents in the way. Instead of trying to force his way through, it's better to turn back shielding the ball, and either pass back or square to a teammate, or to run back a ways with the ball until he has a clear path for a safe pass that will guarantee that possession is kept.

It should be emphasized that square passes have a built in danger. If they are played across in front of defenders, there is a good chance of interception with little recovery room. Square passes should only be made if they are guaranteed safe, and then they should be made crisply and with confidence.

Sometimes to advance you first go back. The tendency of inexperienced players and some experienced players is to go forward regardless of the difficulties facing them. Develop the vision and the self control to make the easy pass back when your forward progress is blocked. Have the patience to use the ball in all directions. Most of this ability comes from using your eyes. Work with the ball until you know where it is well enough to lift your eyes from the floor.

Since keeping possession of the ball is the number one priority, learn to back out of situations where you have little chance of going forward successfully.

By back passing in order to keep possession, you often frustrate your opponents so they lose their poise and start attempting unwise tackles from out of distance, making openings for you to exploit. Careful, patient ball control can often unsettle your opponents so they lose their defensive organization. Remember the back pass when it seems you have no place to go.

The Back Pass (Fig. 42)

(a) White #1 finds his path blocked by Black #1 and #2.
(b) He turns and passes back to White #2.
(c) White #2 dribbles to find passing room to a position where he has several passing lanes open.

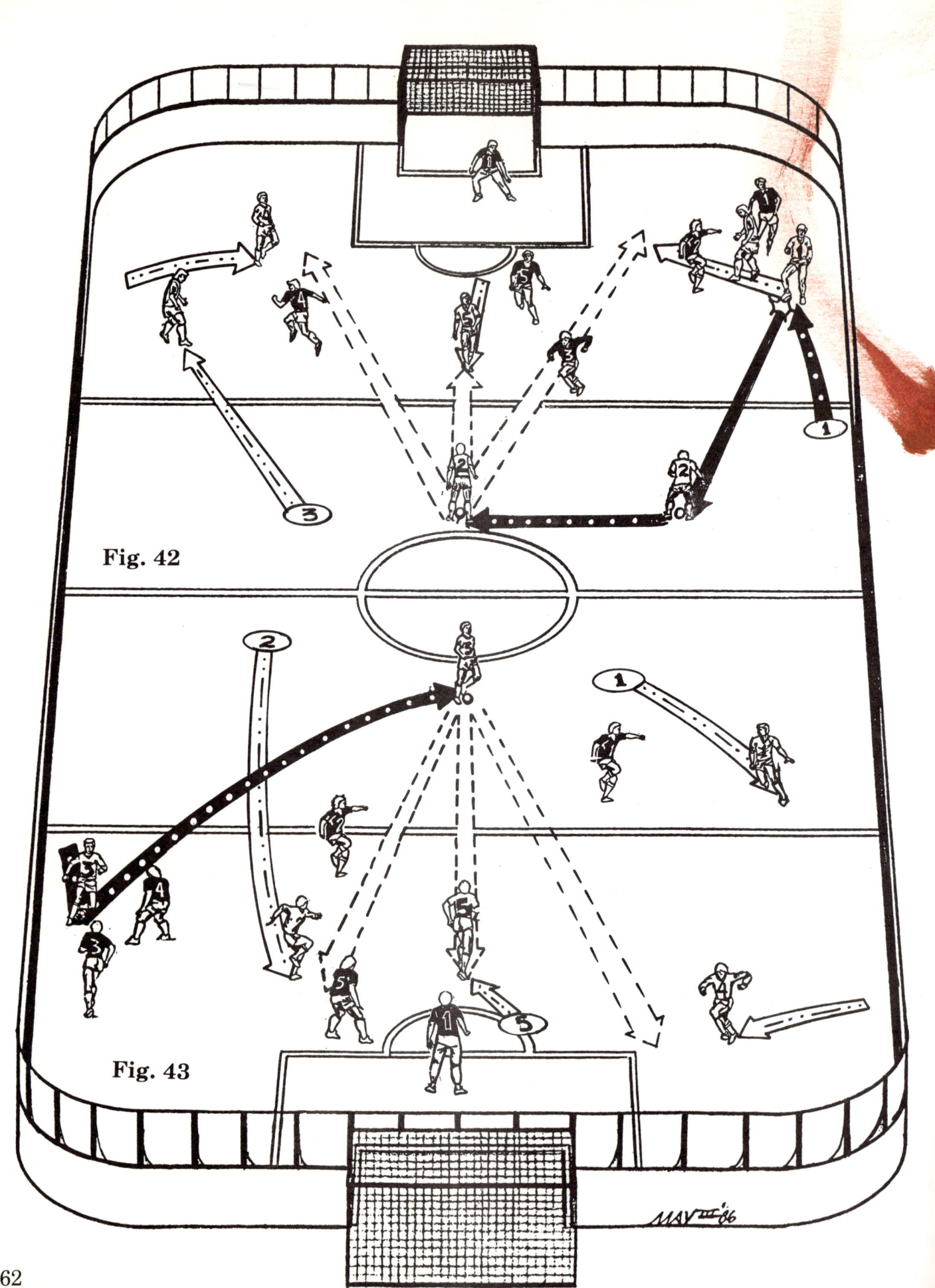

Fig. 42

Fig. 43

The Back Run (Fig. 43)

    (a) White #3 is blocked by Black #3 and #4.
    (b) He dribbles the ball back out of pressure, and finds a spot with open passing lanes to his teammates.

ATTACKING THE FAR POST

Many goals are scored from balls played to the far post. If you play one man forward, he should keep shifting from side to side of the goal, as the ball is passed around the perimeter looking for an opening. The man forward should keep shifting to the opposite side of the goal so that he is always ready to play the ball into goal if it is crossed to him. The keeper has to leave the far corner of the goal unprotected as he moves to cover the threat to the near post. The defenders will mark the forward man tightly, but the urgency and pressure of the play in front of goal will often leave him open momentarily. That's when he gets his name in the paper. Balls to the far post should usually be driven hard for tap in goals.

Attacking The Far Post (Fig. 44)

    (a) The ball is passed around until the defenders are caught out of position.
    (b) After receiving the pass, White #4 beats his man.
    (c) Black #5 comes across to help.
    (d) White #4 slips the ball to White #5 who scores.

Attacking The Far Post (Fig. 45)

    (a) White #2 receives a pass from White #1 and beats his man with a dribble.
    (b) Black #5 comes out to challenge White #2.
    (c) White #5 moves across to the far post to receive a pass and drive it into goal.

Rotating and interchanging of positions is a natural part of the indoor game. It's something all indoor players should realize, so they become comfortable with the quick and constant interchanging of positions that has to go on if an attack is to develop quickly and smoothly, and remain balanced.

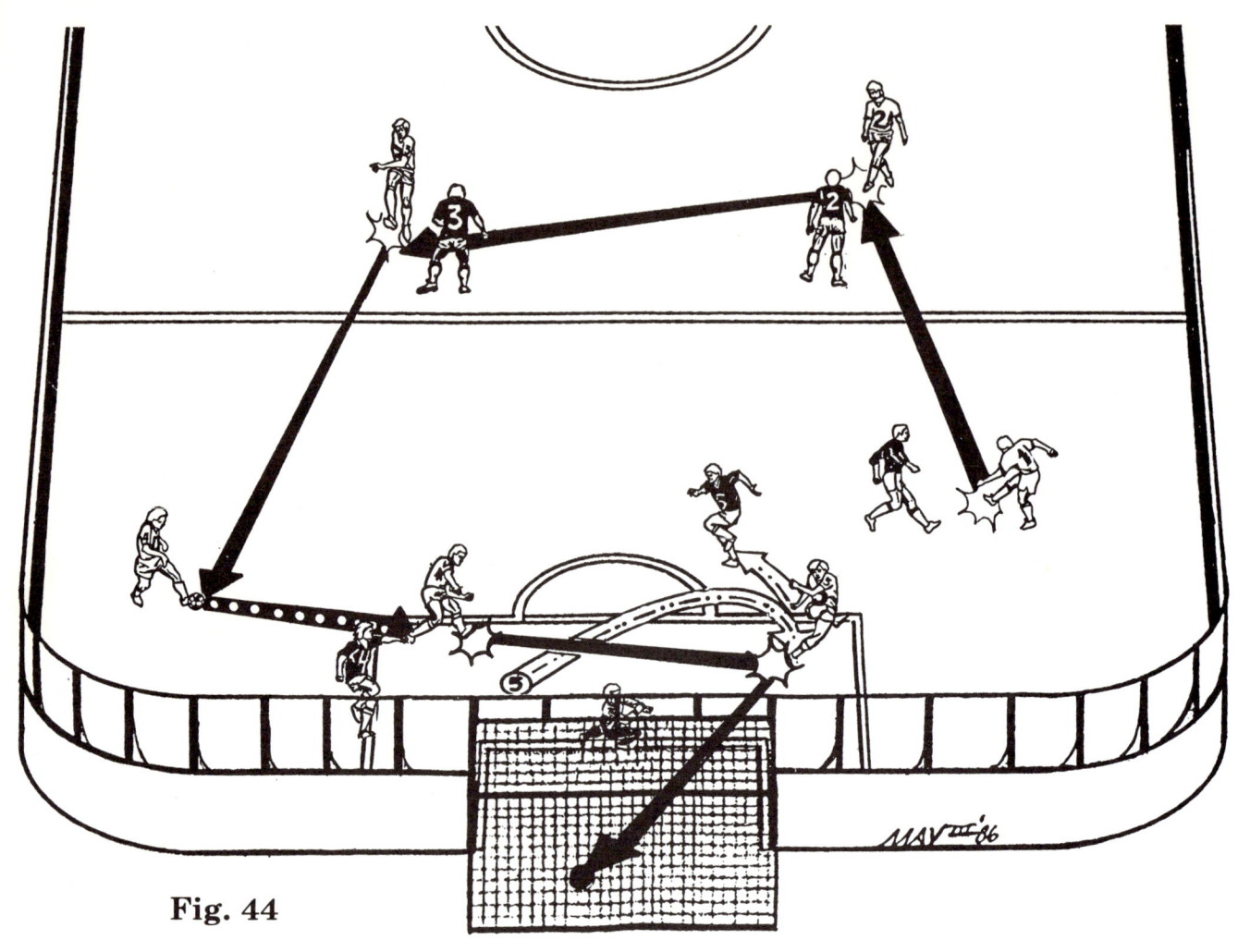

Fig. 44

ONE TOUCH PLAY

At times your play may bog down. All your passes are being picked off. Your opponents seem to know what you are going to do before you do it.

This is a good time for one touch passing. It's assumed you have practiced this as a regular part of your training. Your keep away drills are excellent preparation for one touch passing.

First time passing is difficult, but it has the immediate effect of changing the pace of the game. It speeds up play tremendously, and forces difficult adjustments on the defending players. Professional teams in training spend a lot of time on one and two touch scrimmage.

It requires more alertness on the part of the attackers, and much quicker movement, but if it is well executed, it is nearly unstoppable. You can't maintain one touch passing for long periods of time. Just inject it into your play in spurts of three or four passes at a time to change the pace of play and to unsettle your opponents. Changing the pace of play can devastate a defense. The best way to do this is with one touch passing. One touch play forces you to get your eyes off the floor and see the game better.

Fig. 45

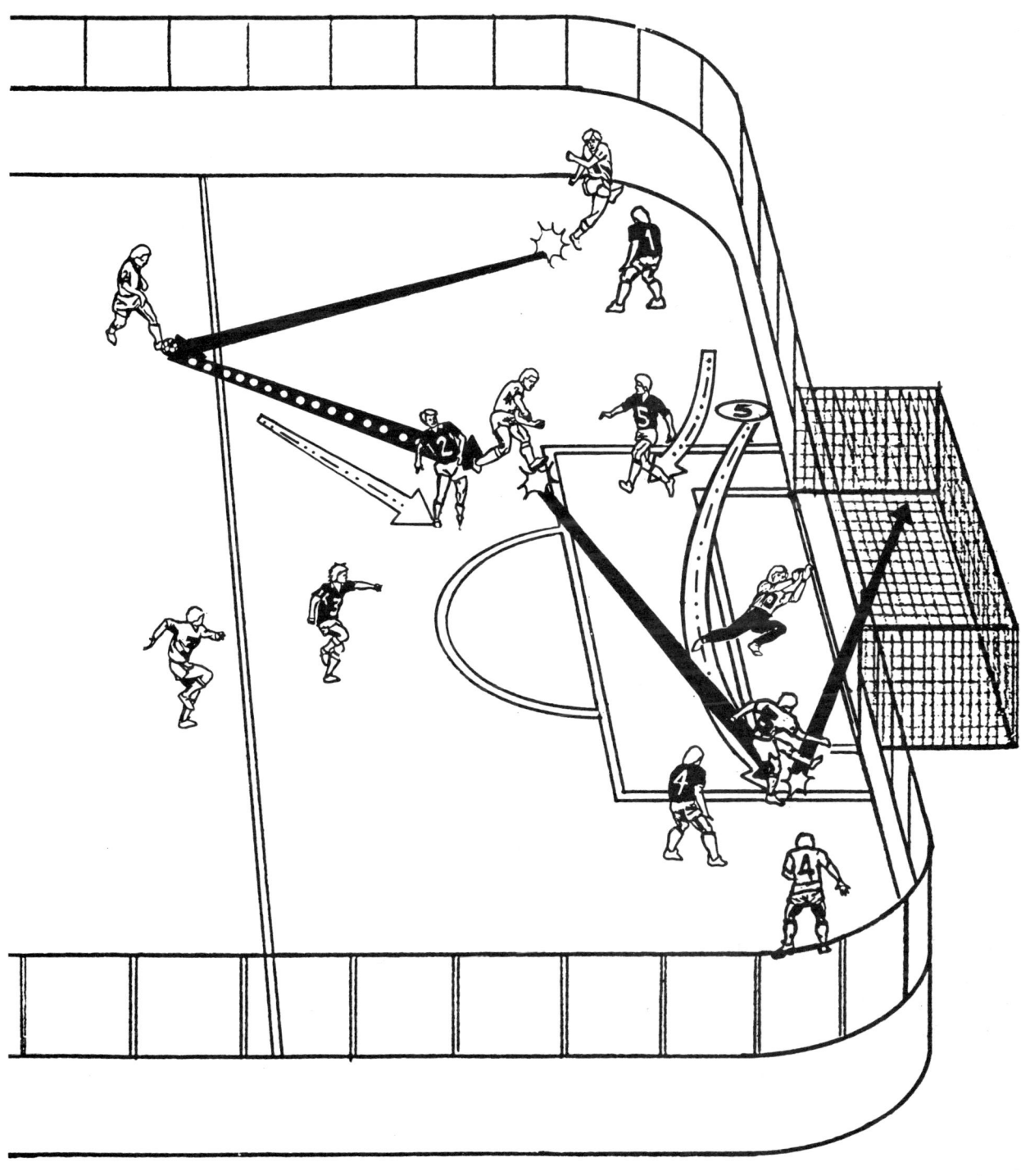

THE GOAL KEEPER IN ATTACK

In Indoor Soccer the goal keeper touches the ball much more than in the outdoor game. When he receives the ball into his hands or to his feet, he starts his team's attack from that point. How he distributes the ball will have a direct bearing on the success of the attack.

Whether he throws long or rolls the ball short will depend on the position of the players on both teams. If he has just stopped a shot on goal, he will be instantly looking for a man in the clear upfield to start a counter attack. If there is no such opening, he may roll the ball short to a defender to start the attacking buildup from there. He can speed up play or slow it down, by the way he handles the ball when it's in his hands.

Some goal keepers seem obsessed with getting rid of the ball quickly. While this may be good if his teammates are ready for it, it will leave them under pressure if they are not ready to receive the ball. The keeper should practice reading the game, so that he can mesh with his teammates, and get a feel for how best to play the ball from his hands. He can set the tempo of the game to a large extent, and is without question one of the most influential players on the field.

The rules prohibit playing the ball in the air over the three lines on the field. Nevertheless, the keeper can throw the ball long as if it were going over the three lines. Instead he throws it to the head of one of his players who then flicks it on to a teammate running by. (see fig. 48)

The man who receives the throw can be standing almost on the third line and still make the throw legal by touching it with his head just before it crosses the third line.

If the play is well executed, it presents an immediate shot on goal.

This is another example of the counter-attack in action, and for success it depends on quick transition from defense to attack, and instant communication between the attacking players, brought about by rehearsing the play.

It's important for a team to develop a "shape" and a system to move the ball on attack, something that works for them. Some moves should become routine as they are proven to work. Don't struggle at things that should come easy. Using the keeper for all he is worth is one of the things that should be routine.

PASSING YOUR WAY OUT AGAINST A FULL COURT PRESS

When all the defenders close down tight in a full court press defense, the goal keeper enters the play as an extra man. He makes sure there will always be an open man to whom to play the ball. He creates 2 on 1 situations to pass out of trouble.

When you're using a target man to stretch the play lengthwise, you might send two players into the attacking half to make criss cross runs, making space for the target man to collect the ball. That leaves your two back players one on one with their markers. It's a two on two game to work the ball out of your defensive zone. Enter the goal keeper. Now it's 3 on 2. The forward attacking players can make their runs with confidence, knowing the three back players should have no trouble bringing the ball up to them. Once the pass is made into the attacking half, the keeper returns to his usual position.

In too many games, the keeper watches his two back players try to work the ball forward under heavy pressure from the two opposing forwards. That pressure could be quickly defeated, if the keeper became part of the passing game. The two back men and the keeper have to be alert in case the opponents send a third man after them. If a third man comes, the attackers have to be ready to pass the ball to the man left open by the third man's move.

No matter how you look at it, the attackers have an extra man in the goal keeper. He should become a planned part of the attack, at least in the defensive zone.

These tactics require the goal keeper to be reasonably skilled with his feet. For amateur teams, it might be easier to make a goal keeper out of a field player than to make a field player out of a goal keeper. The role of the goal keeper indoors is a whole new thing. To use him only as a shot stopper is a great waste, and tactically primitive. He should be able to come off his line and up field to help pass the ball out of the defensive zone with complete safety. If three players can't keep possession of the ball against two defending players with half the field to work in, they need to go back to the keep away game for some more practice. The keeper should join as many foot drills as possible, practice his chip shots and one-two passes. If he becomes skillful with his feet, he adds a new dimension to the attack, and can nullify the full court press, and give his team greater control of the game in their own half of the field.

You should never forget the numerical advantage the keeper gives to the attacking team, but if you don't practice using him in training, you could get into trouble under the pressure of a match.

Passing Your Way Out Against A Full Court Press (Fig. 46)

    (a) Under pressure, White #1 passes back to his goal keeper.
    (b) The keeper dribbles forward drawing the attention of Black #1 who pulls off his man to go after the keeper.
    (c) White #1 makes a run unmolested, and receives the ball from the goal keeper.
    (d) White #2, #3, and #5 make runs to give the keeper other passing options.
    (e) By using the keeper as the spare man, the full court press is defeated.
    (f) Black #1 cannot mark two men at once.

Fig. 46

Fig. 47

Passing Your Way Out Against A Full Court Press (Fig. 47)

(a) Under pressure White #1 passes back to his keeper, then makes a run.
(b) If Black #1 and #2 stay tight with their men, the keeper dribbles forward over the Red line and plays a pass to White #5.
(c) He could also play flighted balls to the corners.

The other attacking players should support the keeper in his movement with the ball, so that he doesn't end up in a vulnerable position with no place to play the ball.

To **Louie Nanchoff** and **Tatu,** forwards for the **Dallas Side Kicks** of the **MISL.**

Question: "What should a team do to overcome the full court pressure defense?" The answers: **Louie Nanchoff:** "I think when you pressure, you're vulnerable to the short passing. If they knock it around, then it opens up the game." **Tatu:** "In that situation you have to play fast and the other players have to **move.** If there is no movement and pressure is applied, the back players try long balls which is what the defenders want." Quick short passes are the answer. Long balls are apt to be intercepted. Speed up play to prevent the defense from adjusting. Try one touch passes. The more skillful the keeper is with his feet, the easier it is to move the ball out of the defensive end.

There should be a reason for everything you do on the field of play. You're in a certain place at a certain time because you have a reason for being there. If you tend to wander without a definite idea in mind, the game flows past you most of the time. When defenders hang back too far away from the play, they leave a gap for the opponents to play into and attack deep near the goal. Either the defenders are trying to rest or they don't know how to play. Resting should be done on the bench. Tactical positioning should be learned in practice time. When you disregard basic principles of passing, control, support, and positioning, you struggle through the game and it becomes very primitive.

THE GOAL KEEPER IN ATTACK:

The Long Throw (Fig. 48)

(a) The keeper throws to White #1 just in front of the red line.
(b) White #1 runs on to the ball and flicks it with his head or foot to White #2.
(c) White #2 runs on and shoots.
(d) White #3 makes a supporting run.

THE GOAL KEEPER IN ATTACK (Fig. 48)

The Long Throw (Fig. 49)

(a) The keeper stops a shot.
(b) He throws long to White #1.
(c) White #1 forms a wedge with the side boards to receive the ball and screen off his defender, and lays the ball back to White #2.
(d) White #2 plays a long ball to White #3.
(e) White #3 gives a wall pass to White #1 who shoots.

Fig. 48

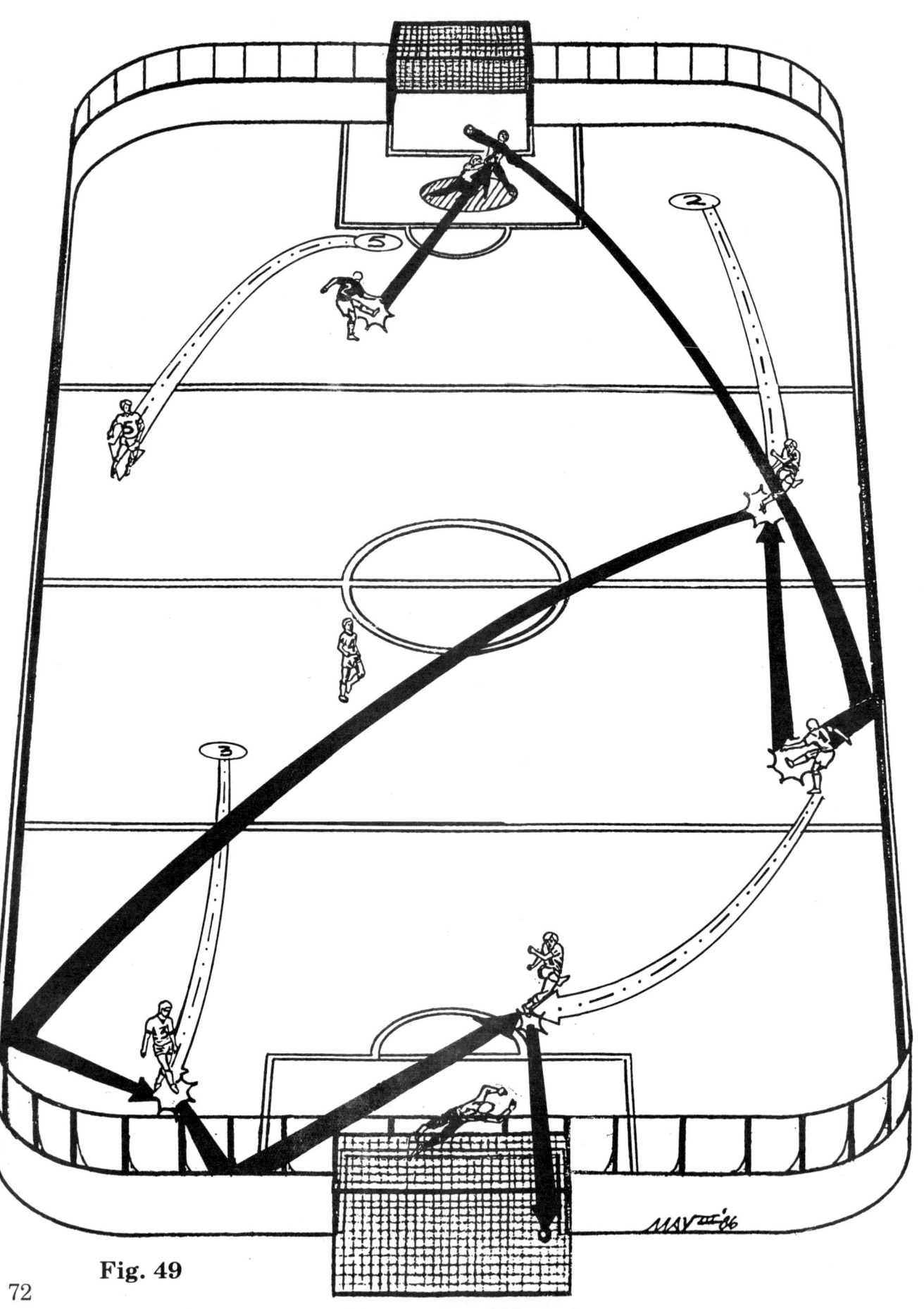

Fig. 49

THE SIXTH ATTACKER

Often when a team is behind in the score and the game is drawing to a close, it's worth a chance at pulling the goalie out from his goal to take part in the attack. If you are faced with a loss anyway, why not take this gamble to increase your chance of scoring.

Sometimes it pays to substitute a more skillful field player for the keeper and let him contribute to the attack. I once watched a professional game where this strategy was used for an entire period. The team was able to pull even and eventually win the match. The skillful use of the tactic put the other team completely on the defensive, physically and mentally, changing the whole complexion and outcome of the match. The player substituting for the keeper should change his jersey and inform the referee of the change in keepers. In indoor terminology he's known as the sixth attacker.

This is a tactic that should be discussed and worked on by the members of your team. It not only adds excitement and variety to your play, but in some cases can pull a game out of the fire for you when all seems to be lost. The other team's history of success against the sixth attacker should be considered.

The success of the sixth attacker play depends on the ability of the attackers to apply enough pressure on the defense to keep them pinned down so tightly they are unable to capture the ball and break forward. Should the defense win the ball, the attackers must instantly double team the man on the ball if possible and quickly funnel back to prevent a counter attack, while the goal keeper heads for his goal to prevent a score.

By playing balls off the boards that rebound in front of goal, the attackers have a good chance of scoring because they have one more man in front of goal than the defenders. **Movement** is the key word. You have an extra man. You have to keep him open by your movement. First time passes are in order here, because the openings exist only momentarily.

The defenders against the sixth attacker play must remain cool and patient and school themselves for an instantaneous counter attack when they get the ball. They must maintain an aggressive and attacking state of mind, even under the extreme pressure of the sixth attacker tactic.

The defenders have to continually shift with the changing positions of the ball, cutting off all passing and shooting lanes.

Goal keepers in the indoor game should give a lot of time to expanding their foot skills. They become more valuable to their team if they can play the ball well with their feet. It's essential for them to be a good attacker when countering a full court press.

As a sixth attacker they will need good passing and receiving skills. One of the relatively undeveloped areas of the game is in the possible uses of the keeper as a field player. Lots of interesting experimentation could take place. Any time you can add an extra field player to your side it's worth some thought.

When the goal keeper advances up field with the attack, he is taking a calculated risk. However, if the run of play indicates a losing situation from which his team will not recover, then he is justified in moving forward as a field player in the attack, since nothing is to be lost, and there is something to be gained.

If he comes forward, he must do it with confidence. It can be very effective. Practice in training will help you learn just how to play this situation. If it works, use it.

The Sixth Attacker (Fig. 50)

(a) White #1 plays the ball to White #2, then it goes to White #3, and back to White #1 who shoots.
(b) Black #4 blocks the shot.
(c) The keeper has come up as a sixth attacker, and collects the ball.
(d) He plays it to White #5 and then supports the attack wherever he is needed.
(e) Obviously if the opponents get the ball, the keeper gets back to the goal as quick as possible.

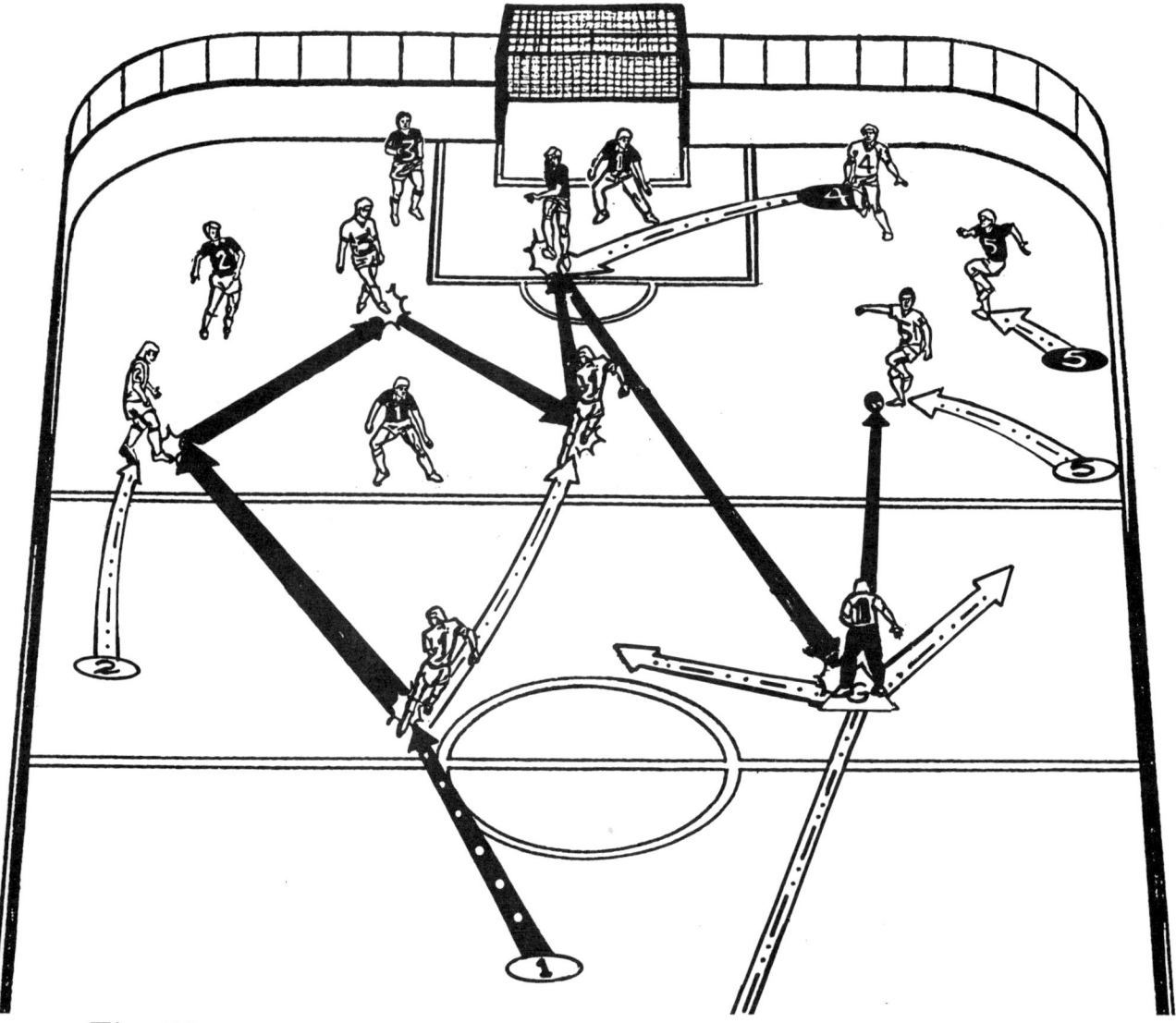

Fig. 50

RETREATING IN ORDER TO ATTACK

The goal keeper can be used to restart attacks that have bogged down in midfield.

When it seems difficult to advance the ball because of tight marking by the opposition, the ball can be dribbled back and passed back to the keeper. If the defenders follow the ball, they will open some space behind themselves. The keeper can then play the ball forward leaving these defenders momentarily stranded and out of the game.

As the attacking team interpass the ball while they drop back toward their own goal, the defending team may be encouraged to go with them in an attempt to get the ball. In that case, the attackers break forward quickly just as the last pass is made to their keeper. They then quickly outnumber the remaining defenders and advance the ball for a shot. This is another example of how intelligent movement can keep your opponents off balance.

Retreating In Order To Attack (Fig. 51)

> (a) Feeling severe pressure, and unable to penetrate the opponents defenses, the White team retreats to reform their attack.
> (b) White #2 dribbles back and passes to White #3, who passes to White #4, who passes back to the keeper.
> (c) As the last pass is made the White team suddenly turns to exploit the space left to them by the advancing Black team.
> (d) A quick series of passes from the keeper to White players #5, #3, and #4, produces a shot on goal off the last pass to White #1.

ISOLATING AN ATTACKER

If you have a back player who's a good attacker, you can isolate him one on one with lots of room around him to beat his defender. Move four of your players to one side of the court taking their defenders with them. Play the ball to the attacker on the weak side, and turn him loose.

You can isolate a player on any part of the court in this way, then try to get the ball to him. This is sophisticated play, but in all your playing and training you should be making habits like this. Most people apply quite sophisticated methods in their jobs. If you apply yourself similarly to your sports, you will get increasing satisfaction.

Isolating An Attacker (Fig. 52)

> (a) All the White Players except White #1 move to the right side of the court taking their defenders with them.
> (b) White #1 makes a sudden sprint to get behind his marker.
> (c) The keeper throws the ball out ahead of White #1.
> (d) He runs onto it, dribbles in and shoots.
> (e) White #5's supporting run gives the ball carrier an option as he nears the goal.

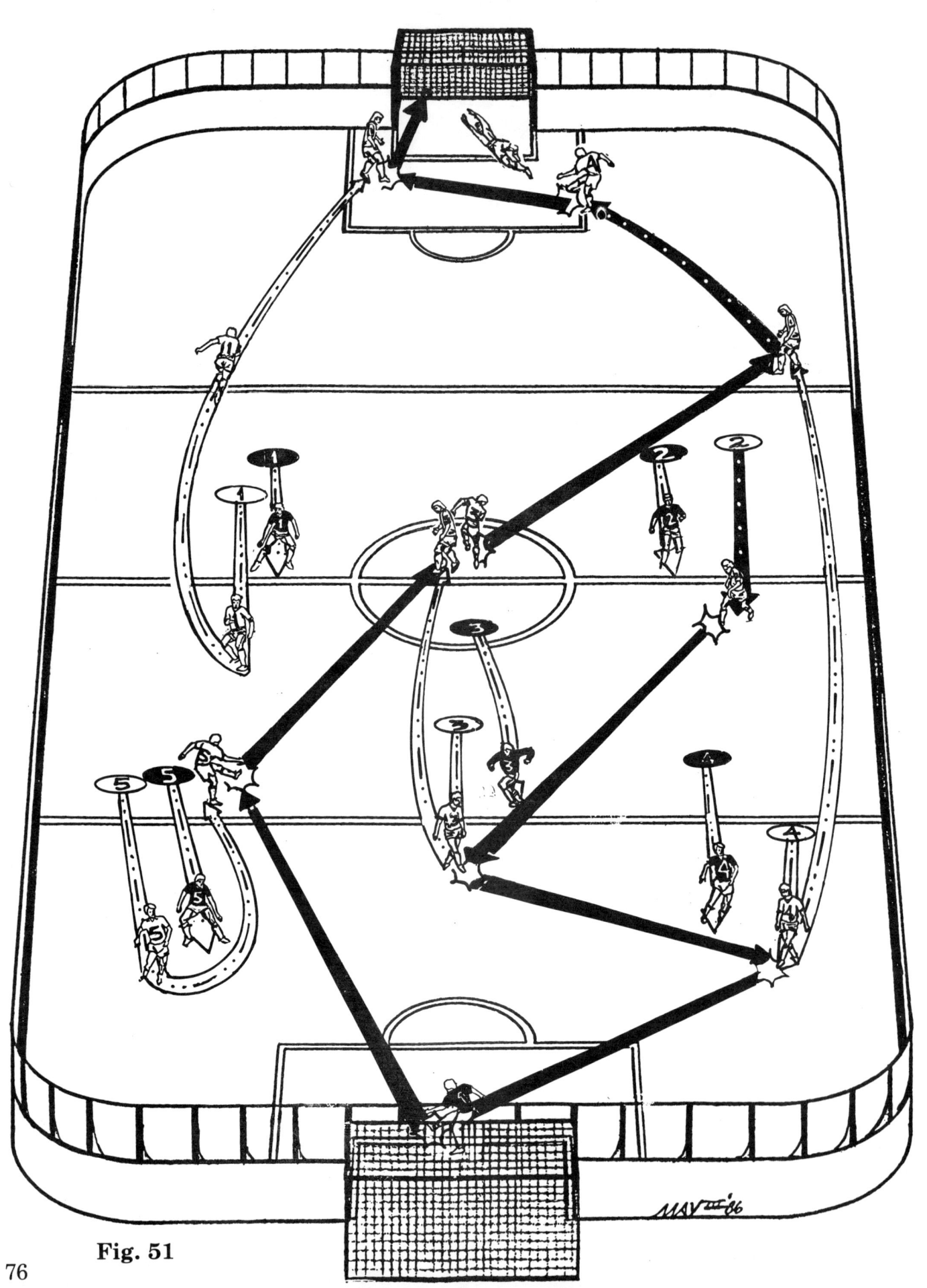

Fig. 51

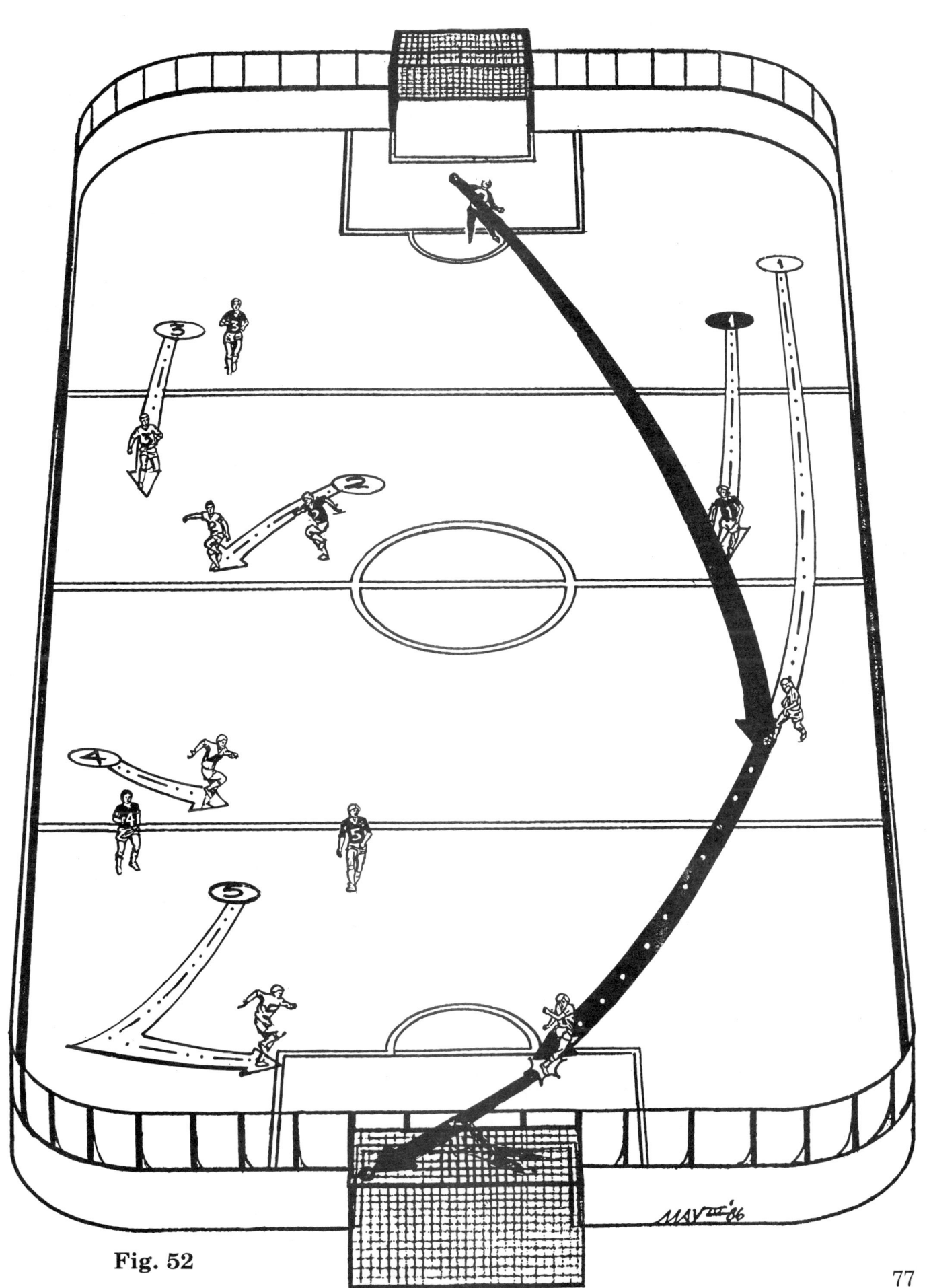

Fig. 52

TRANSITION AND THE COUNTER ATTACK

In basketball they use the term "transition" to describe changes from attack to defense or the change from defense to attack. This transition should take place as **rapidly** as possible. Many teams concede goals in indoor soccer by a slow reaction to losing the ball.

When a team is pressing forward in attack, they can lose possession of the ball with most of their players up near their opponents goal.

If at this time of transition from attack to defense they are slow in reacting and do not drop back quickly to defensive positions, they will find themselves outnumbered and vulnerable. If the other team reacts quickly in counter attacking, there is a good chance that a goal will be scored.

From the Pro's: **Rick Benben,** head coach of the **Kansas City Comets** of the **MISL.**

Question: "What attacking strategies do you try to acquire as a team?"

Answer: "There are two ways you score. You beat the other team down the floor with 2 on 1 and 3 against 2, **counter attacking.** If you can't beat them down the floor, you have to have good **patience** and keep the ball. You have to have a player who can **hold the ball** around the "D" and let players run off him."

"If the defenses are packed in, you have to go around the outside and play balls off the boards."

The counter attack is like the fast break in basketball. It's success depends on quick reaction to a change of possession of the ball. While defending, think ahead to what to do when you capture the ball. Whoever wins the ball, by tackle or interception, should pick out a teammate for an **outlet pass** as far upfield as possible. Everybody else moves to support that pass.

With practice, you can anticipate when the ball will change hands, and be moving to the attack a split second before. The quickness of the transition will leave your opponents flat footed, and you are away toward goal before they can recover. In defense against the counter attack, the people nearest the ball swing back and delay the ball's progress, and wait for help. In vital situations, out-number opponents by quick, intelligent movement.

An attacking team must always be prepared for the possibility of losing the ball. If this should happen, the player nearest the ball immediately closes down on the player with the ball and delays his progress as much as possible. Even a delay of a second or two will allow his teammates to fall back quickly to defensive positions. The reaction from attack to defense must be instantaneous.

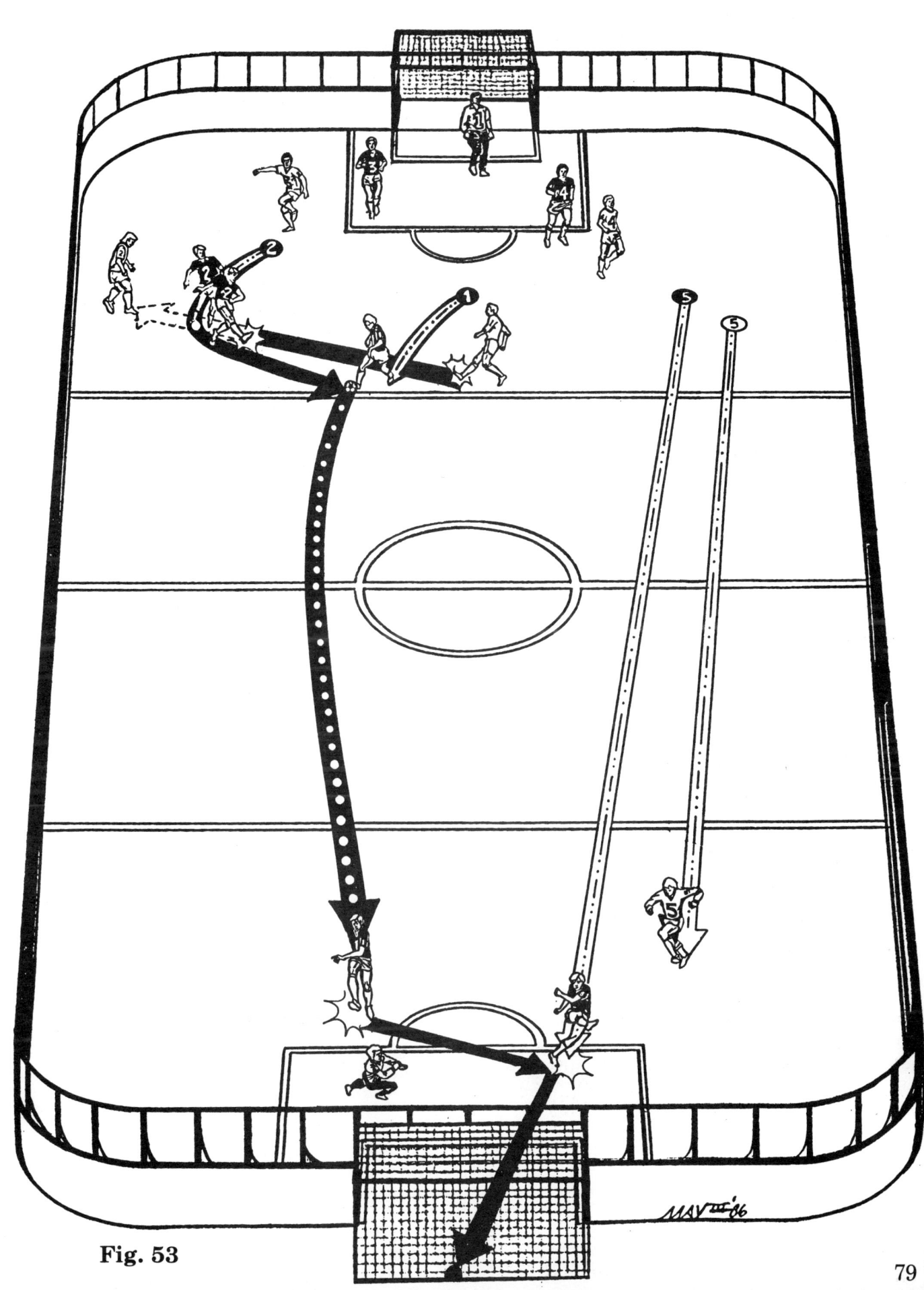

Fig. 53

The positioning of the attacking players can help to keep them from getting caught too far forward. They should avoid a situation where 3 or 4 players find themselves almost in the goal mouth and square to each other. If the defense captures the ball, they can start a counter-attack. It usually ends in a goal scored against you.

It's better for some of the attacking players to play in an arc some yards back from the goal line leaving one or two men right up on the goal if they like. This way it's easy to move on to a ball played toward goal, while at the same time they are nearer to their own goal than the defenders and can quickly fall back to defend, if they lose the ball.

In attacking, a team should develop a "shape" that they feel comfortable with. From this formation players can interchange without losing a basic floor balance from which they can attack and also quickly defend if necessary (see formations of play, page 120).

Ken Cooper: head coach of the **Baltimore Blast** of the **MISL.**

"When we have the ball, we look to break out very quickly with 3v2's and 2v1's, but we always leave one man back as a kind of sweeper."

Transition From Defense To Counter Attack (Fig. 53)

(a) White #1 passes to White #2.
(b) Black #2 intercepts the pass, and immediately plays the ball to Black #1, who has broken clear.
(c) Black #5 reacts to the interception, and makes a supporting run.
(d) Black #1 draws the goal keeper out, and then slips the ball to Black #5 for the score.

Preventing The Counter Attack (Fig. 54)

(a) White #1 and #2 can both see that the pass to White #2 is going to be intercepted.
(b) They immediately get goalside of their opponents to slow down the counter attack, and to give their teammates time to take up defensive positions.
(c) This quick reaction to a change of possession has prevented the counter attack from developing.

A team's counter-attacking ability is directly related to it's substitution policy. To be ready and able to defend back the length of the court, and then break forward in a flash, to run the length of the court in a counter attack, requires fresh legs. You can only maintain fresh legs by frequent substitutions.

Fig. 54

The Counter Attack (Fig. 55).

    (a) The attackers have been caught too square to each other too close to the goal.
    (b) White #4 takes a shot.
    (c) The keeper stops the shot.
    (d) The defenders react quickly and sprint up field.
    (e) The keeper throws to Black #4.
    (f) The attackers are left stranded.

Preventing The Counter Attack (Fig. 56)

    (a) White #1 passes to White #2 who shoots on goal.
    (b) The keeper stops the shot, but must be content to roll the ball short to Black #3.
    (c) Playing in an arc further from goal, the White players can recover better if they lose the ball, and fall back safely to defensive positions.

Fig. 55

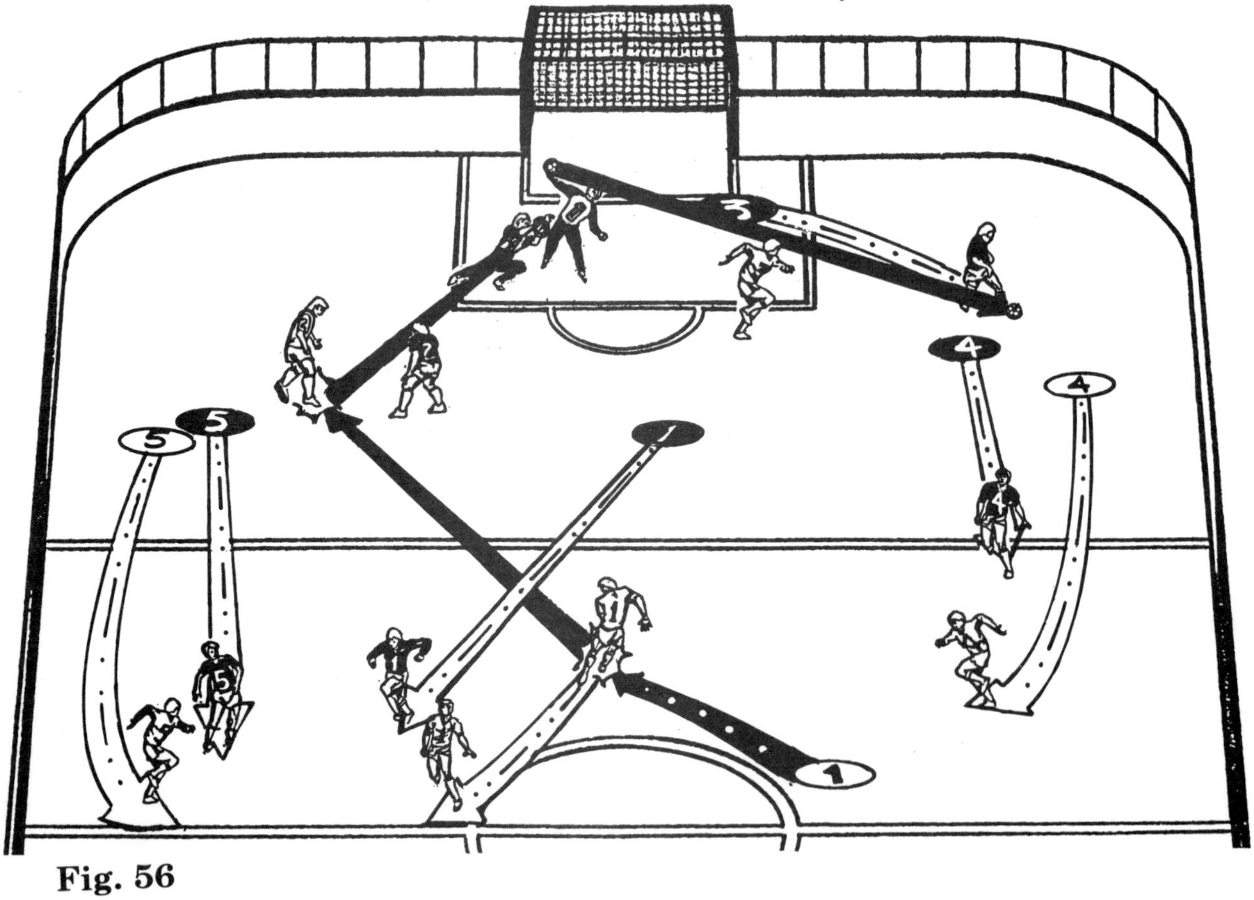

Fig. 56

When defenders make runs with or without the ball, forwards have to track them down. There's no one else to do it. Everybody's occupied with his own man.

If a defender intercepts the ball deep in his own end, the forward for whom the pass was intended is the only one left to match up with the man on the ball. That's because his teammates, trying to prevent a counter attack, have all matched up with their corresponding opponents.

If the forward doesn't chase him, the defender, who now has the ball, will have a clear path to goal, if his teammates move intelligently. (they have to run off the ball in a way that will take their markers out of the way of the ball carrier.)

Often when the defender intercepts the ball, he'll have a head start on the forward trying to track him down. Never-the-less, the forward has to chase him, and at least limit his movement and hope for help from a quick thinking teammate. If the forward doesn't chase him, the counter attack has an extra man. A lot of goals are scored from this situation.

As an attacker, you have to be wary of this possibility. As a defender, you have to take advantage of it.

Another word about the counter attack. The aim is to outnumber the defenders with a quick thrust. Even if you have even numbers, the quick thrust can can still have an advantage. It's easier to attack with 2 on 2, or 3 on 3, than it is with 4 on 4 or 5 on 5 because you have more room to play.

COUNTER ATTACK DRILLS

In these drills the defensive players (black jerseys) become the attackers as soon as they have the ball. The length of the field should be adjusted to the speed, skill, and age of the players. Use any distance from half court to full court. Set a time limit on the counter attack to encourage direct movement toward the goal. Vary the time limit to suit the speed, skill, and age of the players. Try five to fifteen seconds. Use whatever time limit forces the attackers to drive on the goal as directly as possible. In these drills keep rotating players until everyone has had at least one chance at every position.

The keys to counter attacking are: the speed of transition from defense to attack; the timing and direction of any passes made; the dribbling skills to beat opponents one on one when necessary; and the directness with which the counter attackers pass or carry the ball into the primary space, the dangerous spots around the goal.

Counter attacking drills are probably the most important drills you can practice, since so many goals are scored this way in matches.

Counter Attacking Drill: One on One (Fig. 57)

(a) The distance between White #1 and Black #1 is approximately three feet.
(b) To start the drill, White #2 plays the ball to Black #1 to simulate an interception, and then moves out of the play.
(c) White #1 and Black #1 must remain in place until the ball reaches Black #1.
(d) Black #1 receives the ball and breaks for the goal.
(e) White #1 has to sprint hard trying to catch Black #1 and get goalside of him and the ball.
(f) If Black #1 beats White #1 to the goal, he tries to score.
(g) If White #1 gets goalside first, they go one on one until a score is made, or time runs out.

Counter Attacking Drill: Two Against One (Fig. 58)

(a) To start the drill, White #1 plays the ball to Black #2 to simulate an interception.
(b) Black #2 dribbles the ball forward as White #1 retreats staying goalside trying to slow down the play.
(c) Black #1 spreads the play, and runs forward to receive the pass.
(d) White #1 continues to retreat and delay the play hoping for help.
(e) Black #1 and Black #2 continue creating two against one, attempting to produce an open shot on goal.
(f) This is a hypothetical play showing what might happen. When the players run through this drill, the play of the Black players will depend on how White #1 reacts to their passes and moves.
(g) In theory, the Black players should spread out, with the man on the ball attacking White #1, and the other Black player trying to find a position where he can receive a pass **behind** the defending White player.
(h) The defending player, White #1 has to avoid being drawn away from the middle, because the attackers can then beat him with a pass to the center, and have a clear path to the goal. He should try to force play to the outside and keep the play in front of him as much as he can without being drawn out himself. The attackers should play as fast as possible, because in a full size game White #1 could expect help from his teammate.
(j) Play continues until a goal is scored, possession is lost, or time runs out.

3 on 2 Counter Attack Drill (Fig. 59)

(a) White #1 plays the ball to Black #1 to start the drill.
(b) Black #1 plays the ball to Black #2 to start the counter attack.
(c) Black #1 and #3 make attacking runs as black #2 starts his dribble.
(d) White #1 gets goalside of Black #2 trying to slow down the play.
(e) White #2 makes a defending run trying to slow down and contain Black #3.
(f) If White #1 stays with Black #2, Black #2 passes to Black #1 who takes the shot.

If White #1 pulls off Black #2 in order to mark Black #1, Black #2 takes the shot on goal.

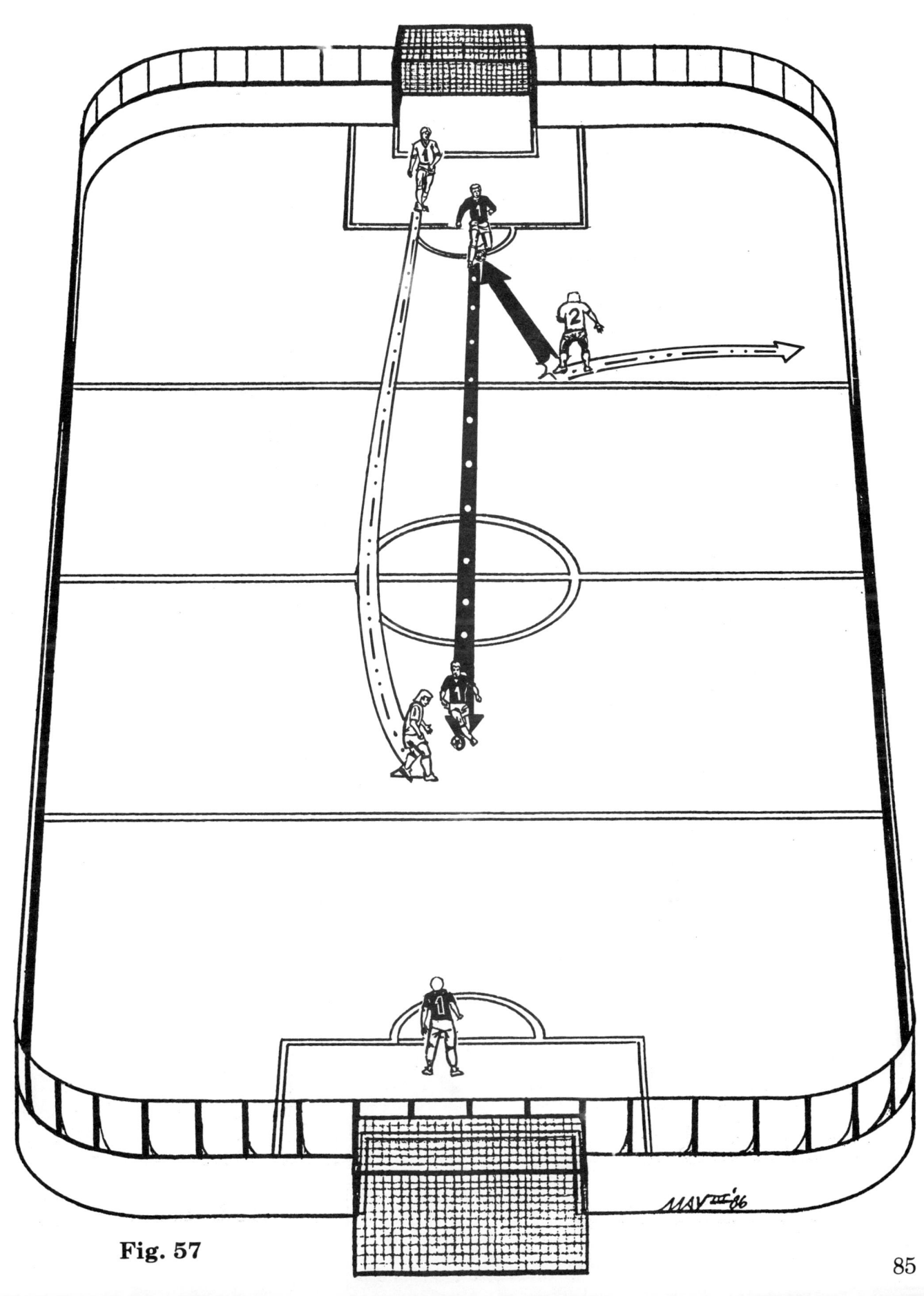

Fig. 57

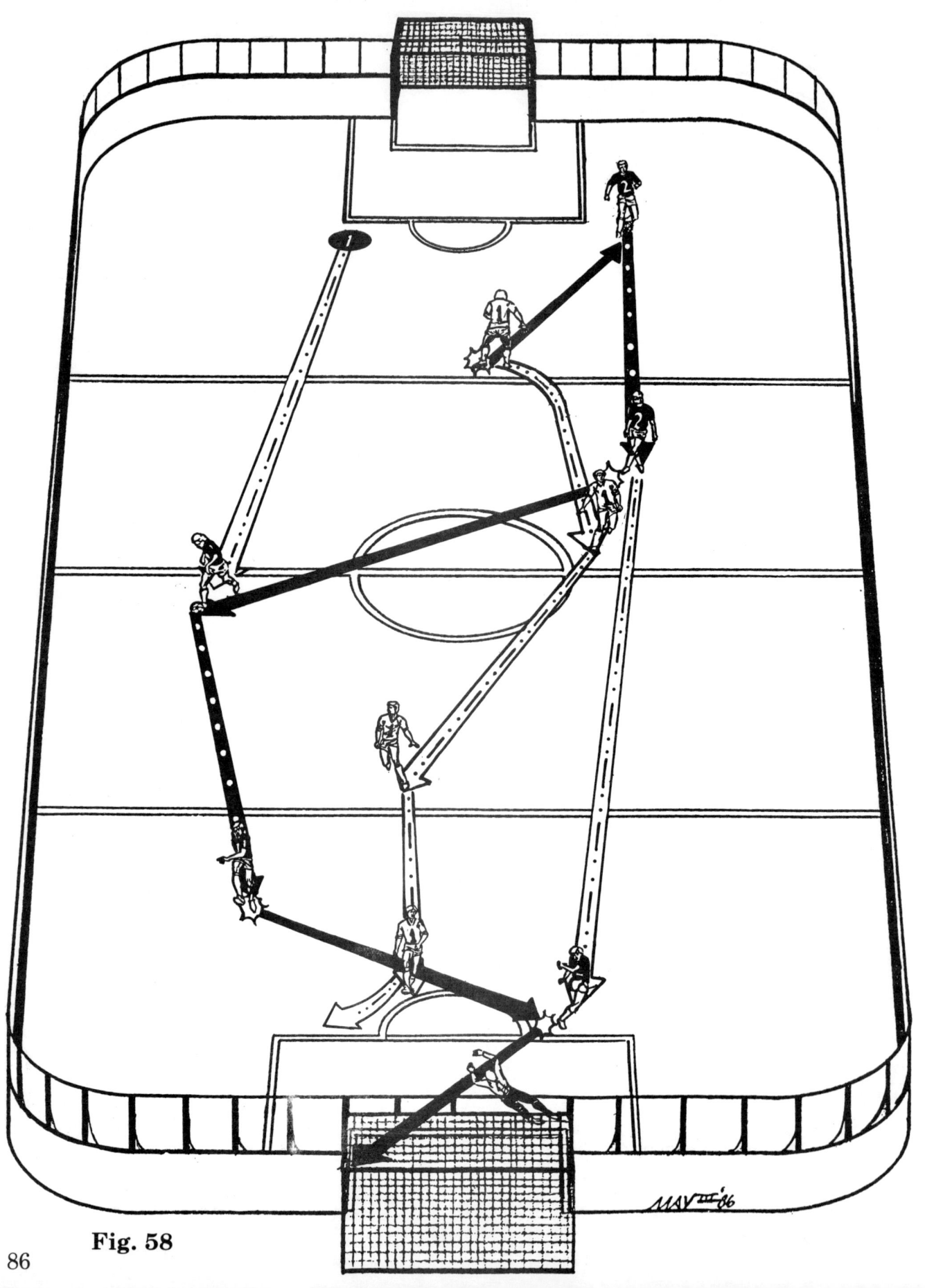

Fig. 58

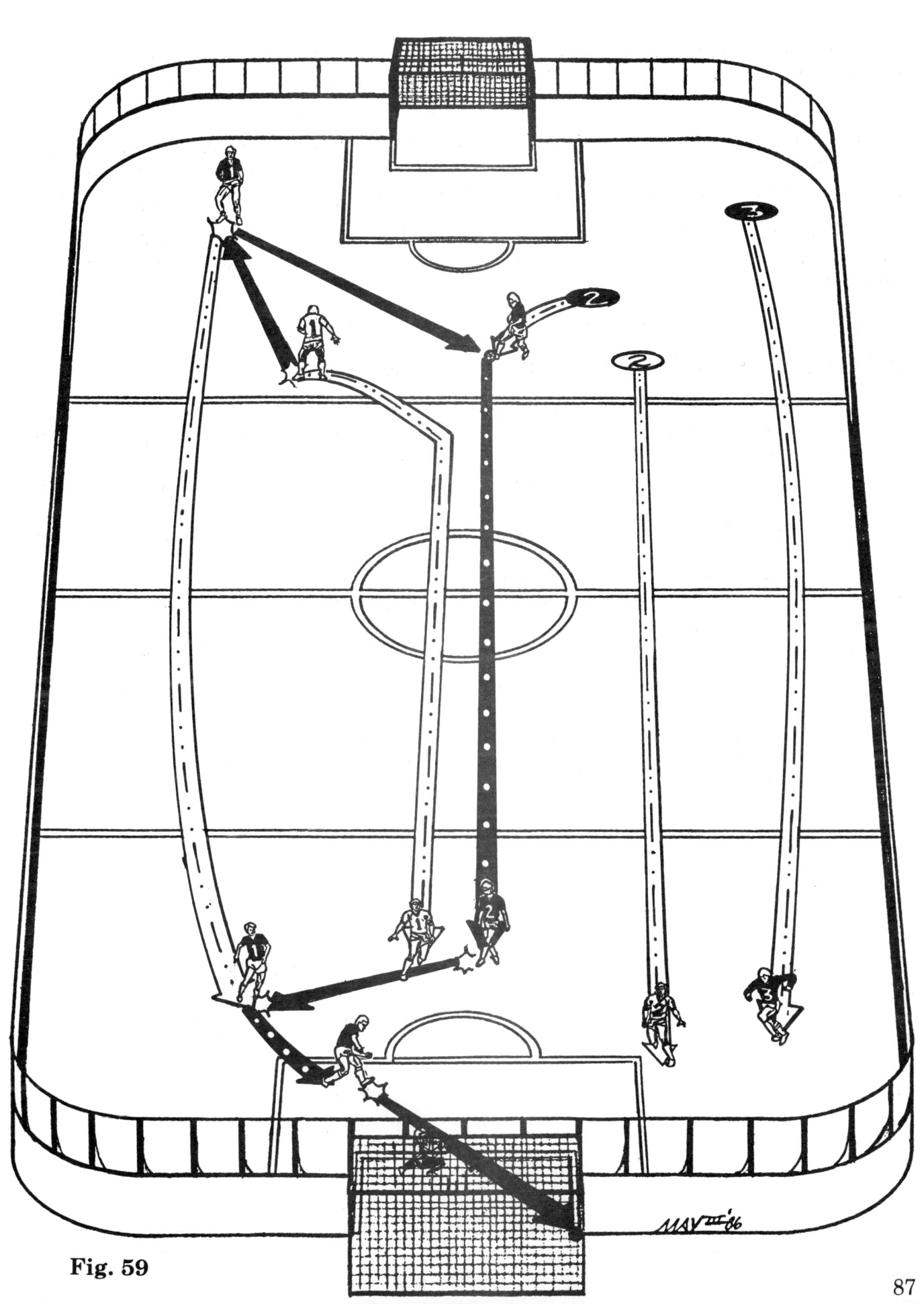

Fig. 59

The Black players interpass the ball with each other if necessary, but try to get the ball to the center man Black #2 as they near the goal, since that will give them more options to score.

If the two White players can force the ball to be passed to the outside as the Black players near the goal, they have a better chance to capture it or block a shot, because the angle will be tougher and the man left open will be as far away from the ball as possible.

During the drill, the attackers and defenders have a chance to explore many different runs and passing patterns, and will eventually discover what works best for them in this situation.

Use a time limit to force a direct attack on the goal.

Drill: Try To Score One On One Plus The Goal Keeper (Fig. 60)

(a) Defender, Black #1 plays the ball to attacker White #1.
(b) White #1 then has five seconds to try to score against Black #1 and the goal keeper.
(c) Replace Black #1 with another player who starts the drill again by playing the ball to White #2.
(d) Continue the drill until everyone has a chance at all positions, for as long as desired.
(e) Vary the time limit to suit the skills of the players. Assign the stop watch to a player so the coach or advisor can criticize the drill.

Drill: Try To Score One on One Against The Goal Keeper Only (Fig. 61)

(a) Use the same procedure as the preceding drill, except the keeper plays the ball to the attackers to start the action.
(b) Alternate goal keepers if you have more than one. Field players can also play in goal, since in recreational matches this often happens. It's also good experience for sixth attackers.

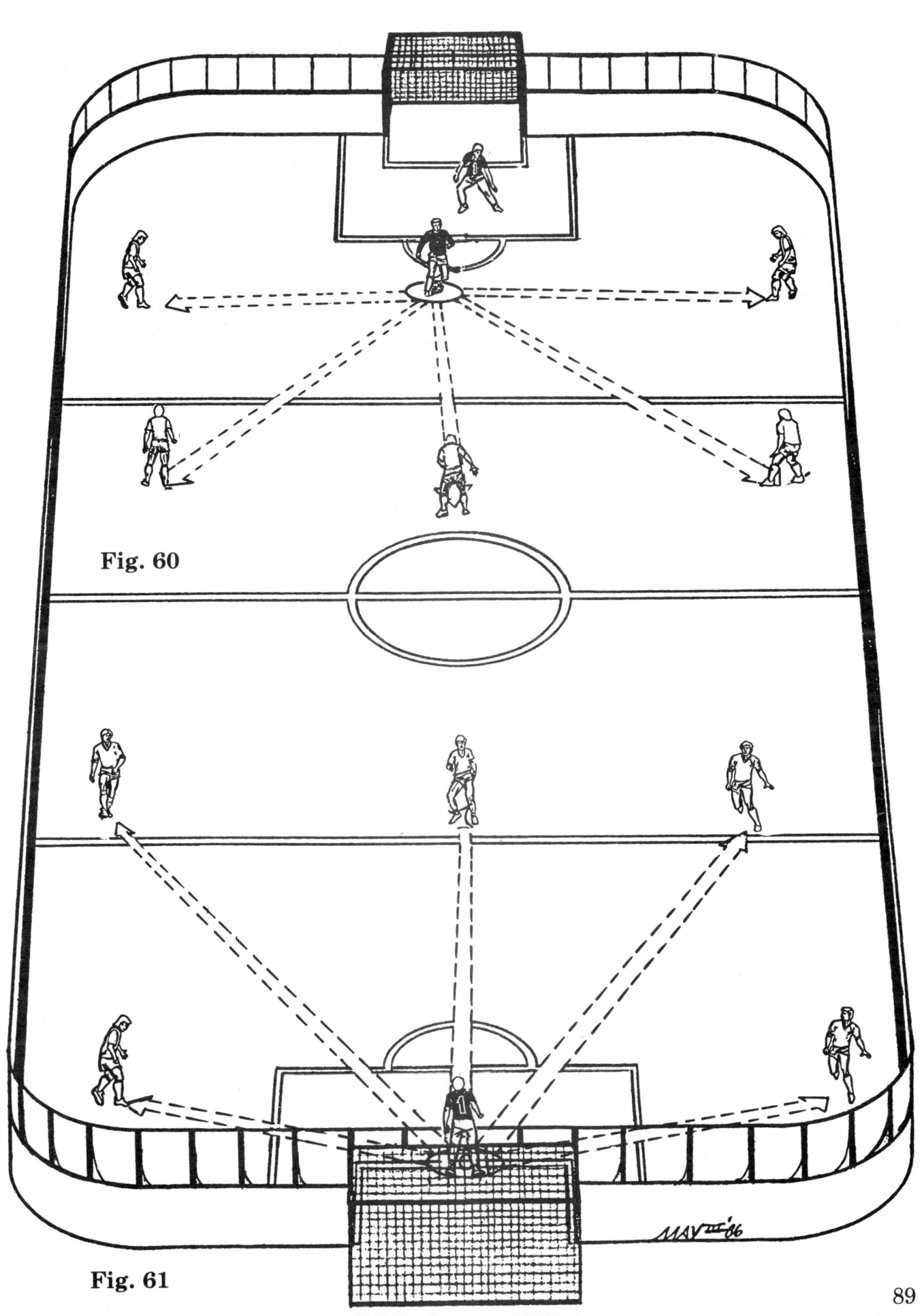

Fig. 60

Fig. 61

SET PLAYS FROM DEAD BALL SITUATIONS

Each dead ball play near goal is a golden opportunity to score. Most of the time the opportunity is lost because of lack of preparation. Remember, you don't have to wait for a whistle to take a free kick or an inbounds pass. This means alert attackers can play the ball quickly sometimes, before the defenders can adjust and mark their opponents.

Many goals are scored by taking the kick quickly and using the element of surprise. When this is not possible, a team must have several trick set plays to use to create an opening for a good shot. (see diagrams for several possible plays)

By having these plays, you can vary your use of these valuable opportunities instead of just blasting the ball at goal and hoping for the best. It's best to keep these plays simple, and practice them enough so everyone in the team knows his role in their execution. You can give each play a number, and then call it out before the play. You can disguise it by calling more than one number, making the second or third number the real one.

Walk through these plays first, to get the hang of them without defenders. Then try them at ½ speed, still no defenders. When you can make the play at game speed, introduce passive defenders who take up defensive positions but don't try to tackle or intercept the ball. When you thoroughly understand the play, the defenders can become more active. Since the defenders will know what the attackers are going to do, the attackers will have to be ready to deceive them by running another set play instead. It takes a lot of practice to make these set plays work, but if your reward is a goal, the work is worth it. The more versatile your game, the more effective it will be, and the more fun you will get out of the game.

Practice your set plays until the timing and understanding by the players is perfected. Then when the situation comes up in a game, the whole thing will work.

Lots of goals are scored by professionals in what look like on-the-spot invention. Actually it is often the players responding to a situation that has been practiced many times over in training.

Confidence is having done the thing before. Don't ever become bored by repetition. Repetition is the only sure learning process.

The thrill of making a combination work in a game after having practiced it in training is reward enough for the effort. Ballet dancers rehearse and rehearse combinations of steps, until they can perform them flawlessly. In soccer you have to do the same, but it's more difficult because six other players are out there trying to prevent your doing it.

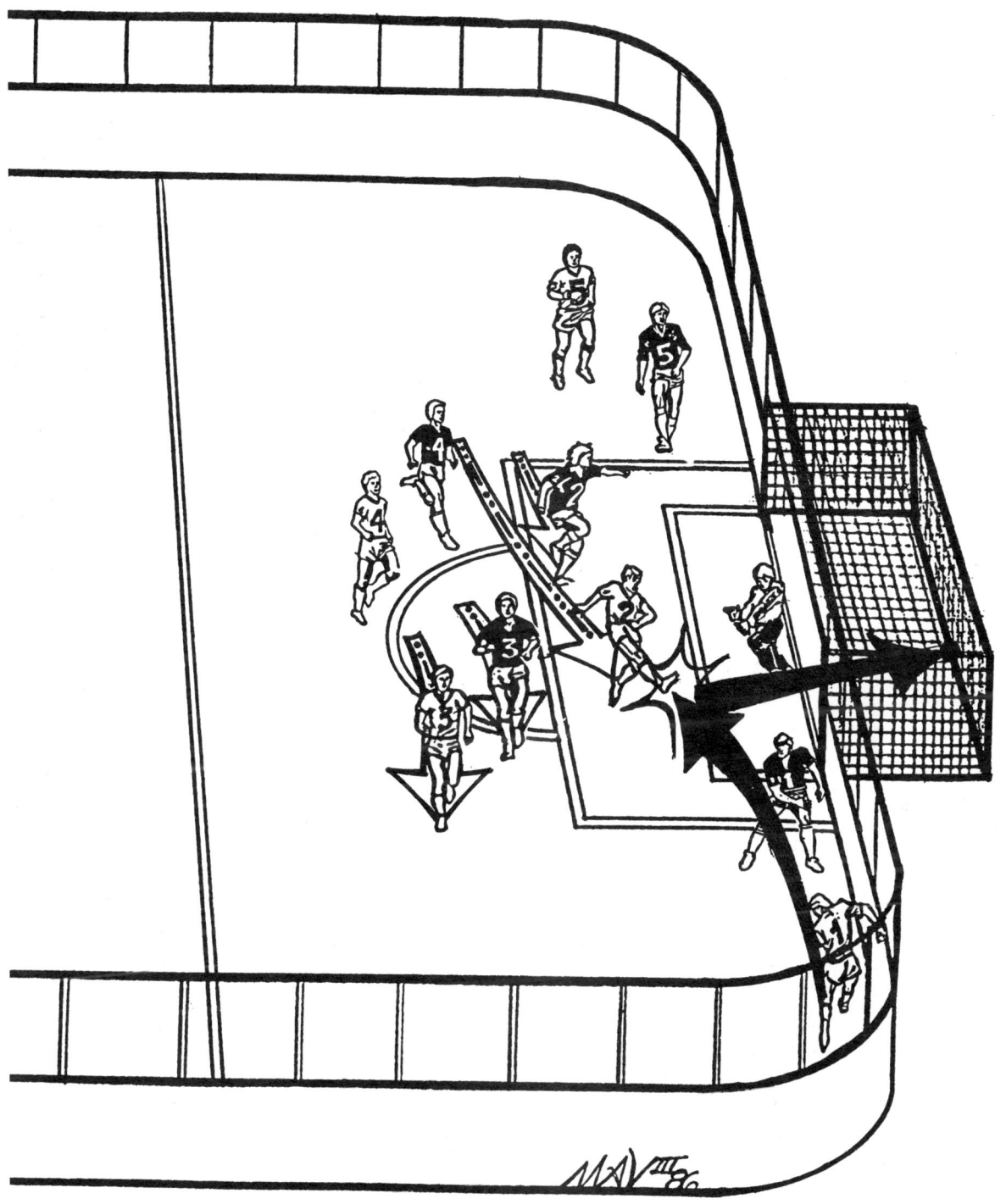

Fig. 62

Corner Kick Set Play (Fig. 62)

    (a) White #3 makes a decoy run to take his marker away from the play.
    (b) White #2 times his run to get in front of Black #2 for the first touch of the ball.
    (c) White #1 times his pass to arrive simultaneously with White #2, who deflects the ball first time into the net.

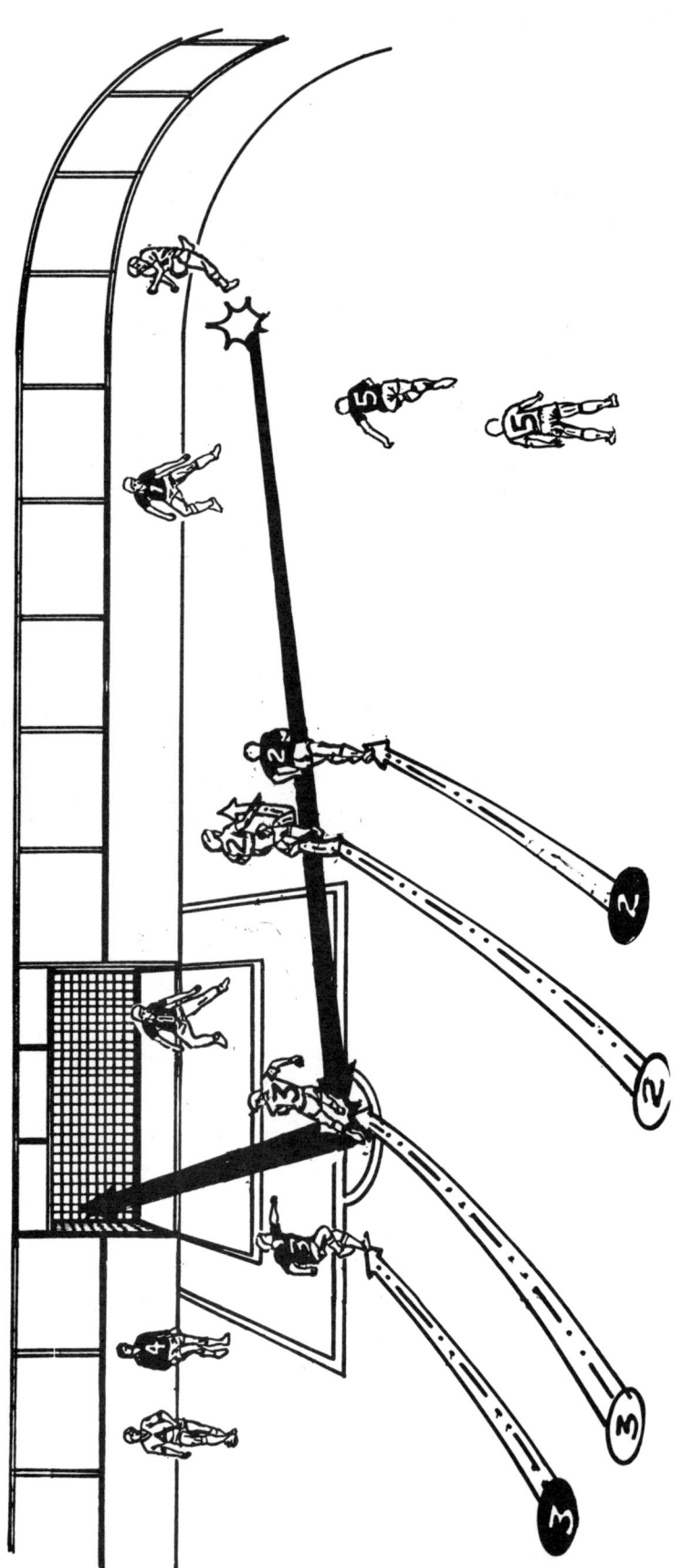

Corner Kick Set Play (Fig. 63)

(a) White #2 starts his run and gets ahead of his marker Black #2.
(b) Instead of playing the ball he steps over it leaving it for White #3.
(c) White #3 times his run to meet the ball and shoot first time.
(d) The false run by White #2 draws the goal keeper to the right to give White #3 an open net to the left.

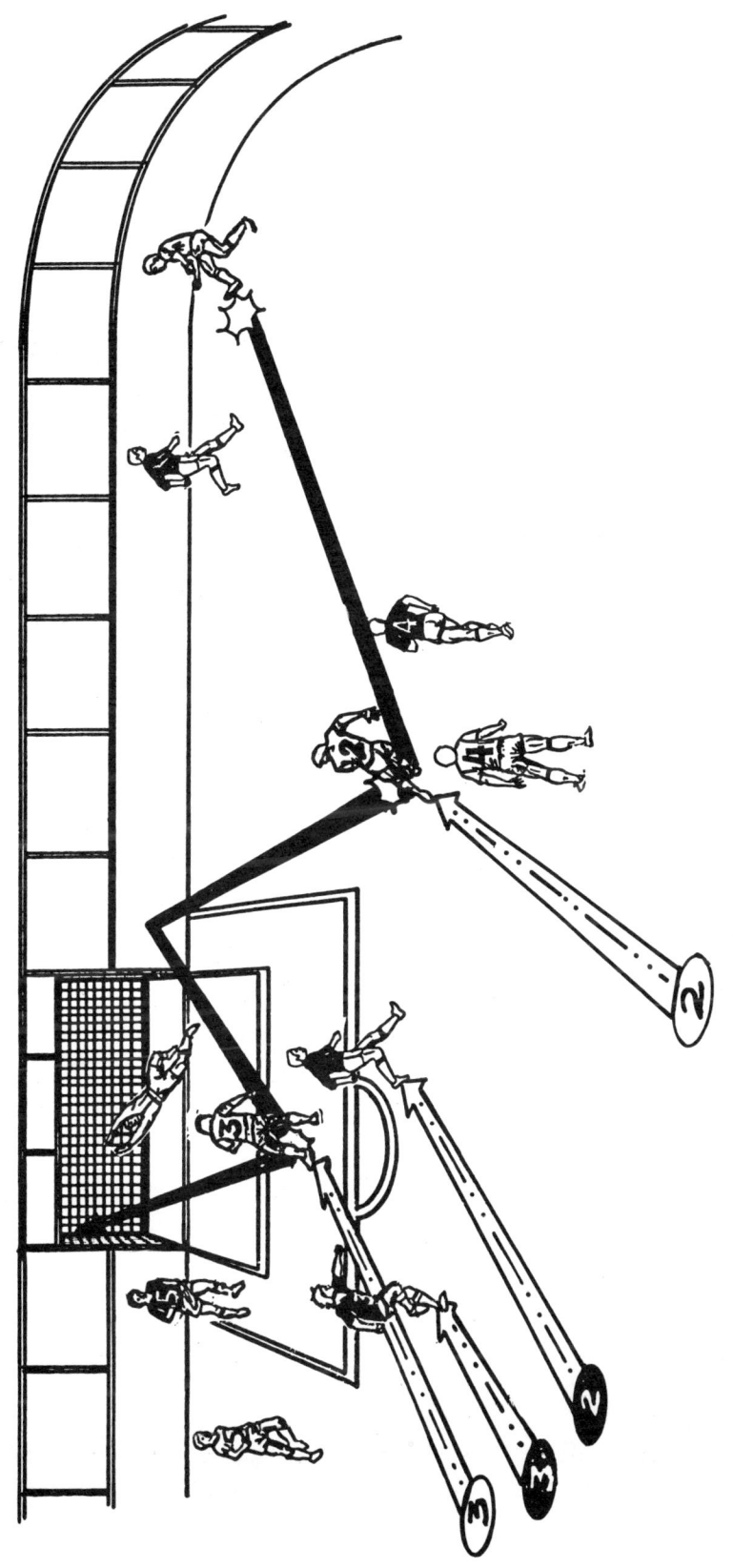

Corner Kick Set Play (Fig. 64)

(a) White #1 plays the ball to White #2.
(b) White #2 plays a wall pass to White #3 who shoots.
(c) White #2 and #3 have to coordinate their runs perfectly.

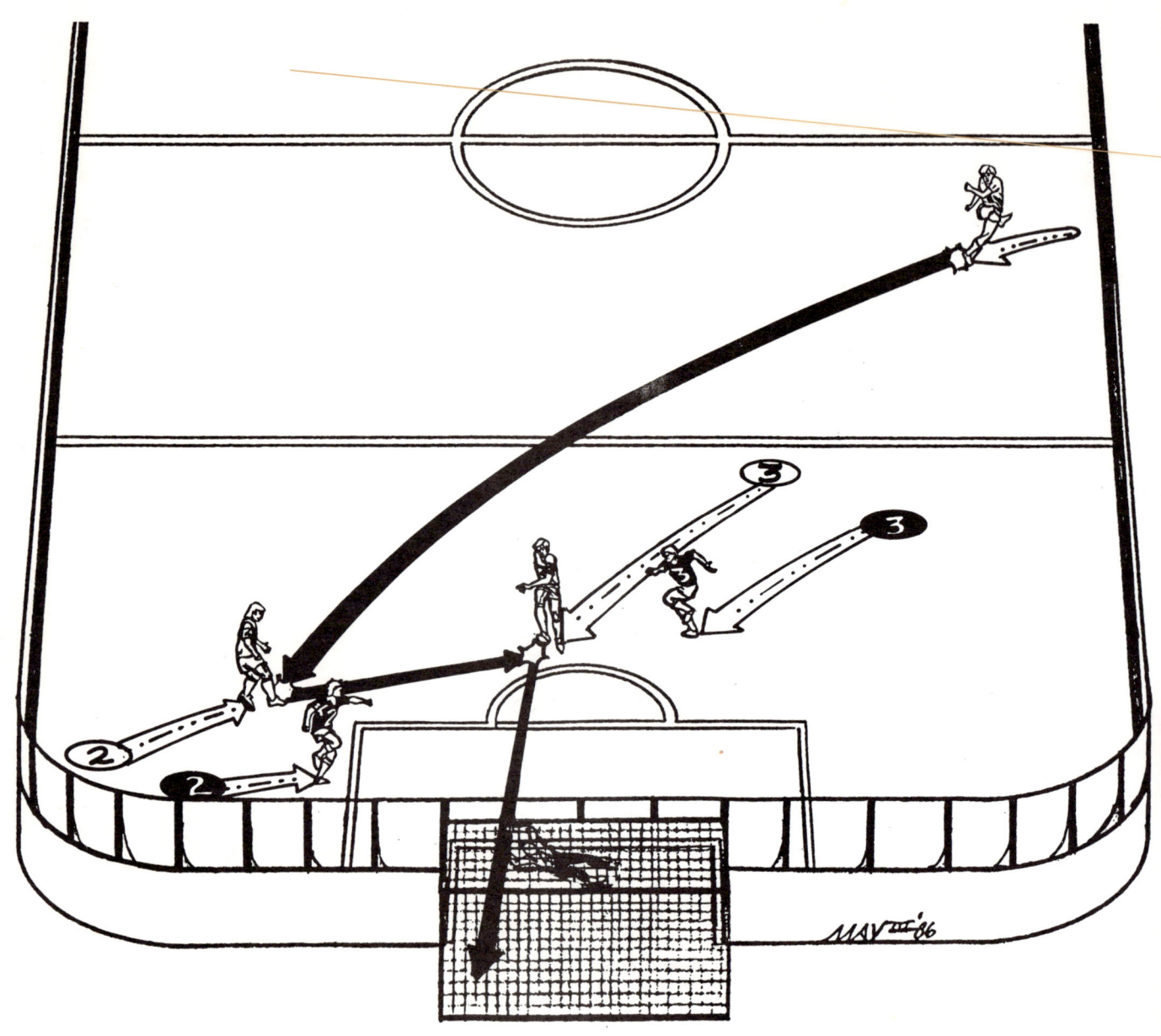

Free Kick Set Play (Fig. 65)

    (a) White #1 chips the ball to White #2.
    (b) White #2 plays the ball **down** for White #3 to finish with a shot on goal.
    (c) White #2 and #3 have to time their runs just right if the play is to work.

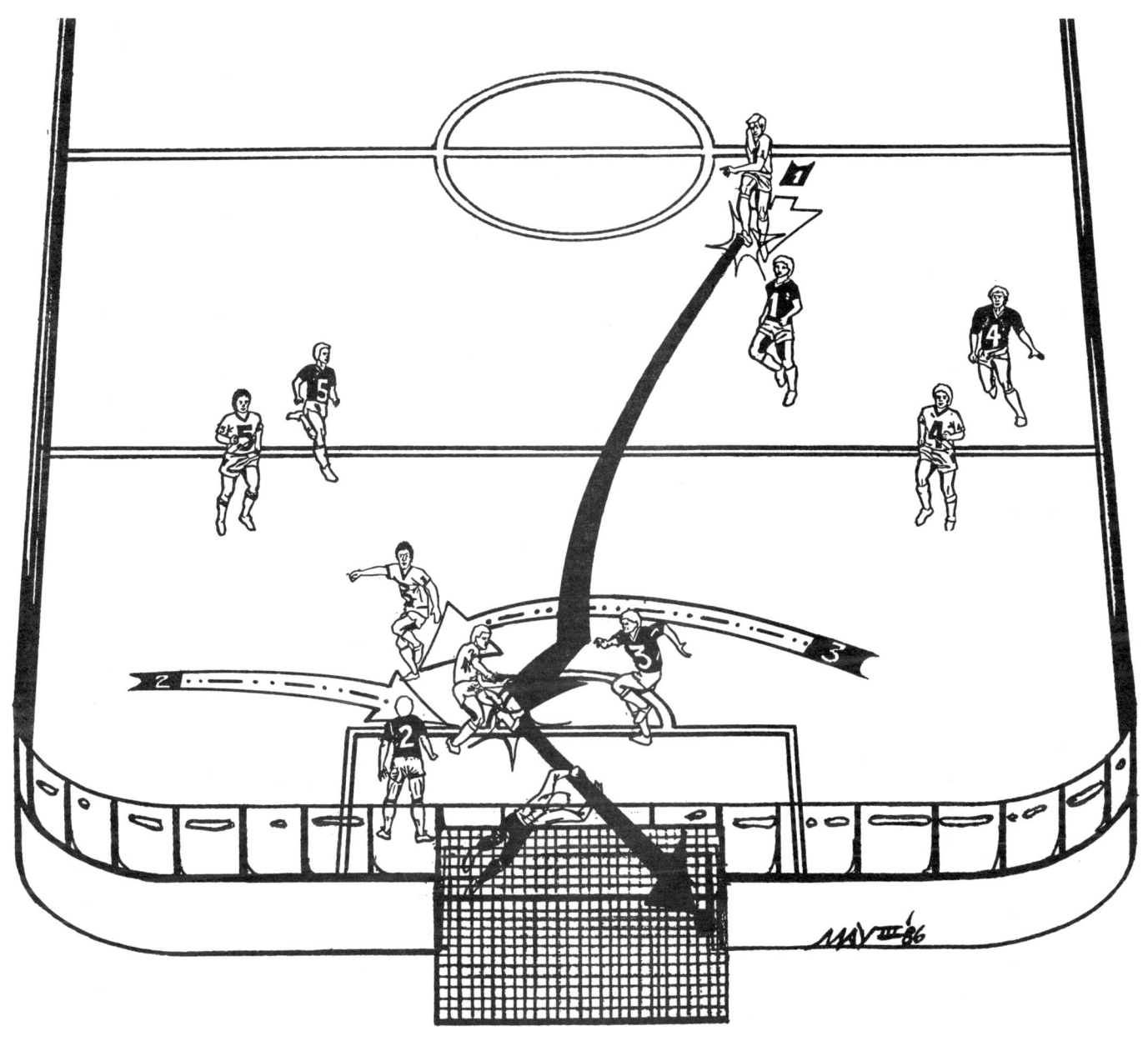

Free Kick Set Play (Fig. 66)

    (a) White #1 tries to play the ball to the most advantageous spot.
    (b) White #2 and #3 make criss cross runs in the hope that one of them can make contact with the ball and flick it into the goal. The ball can be lofted for a header or played on the floor for a deflection by foot.

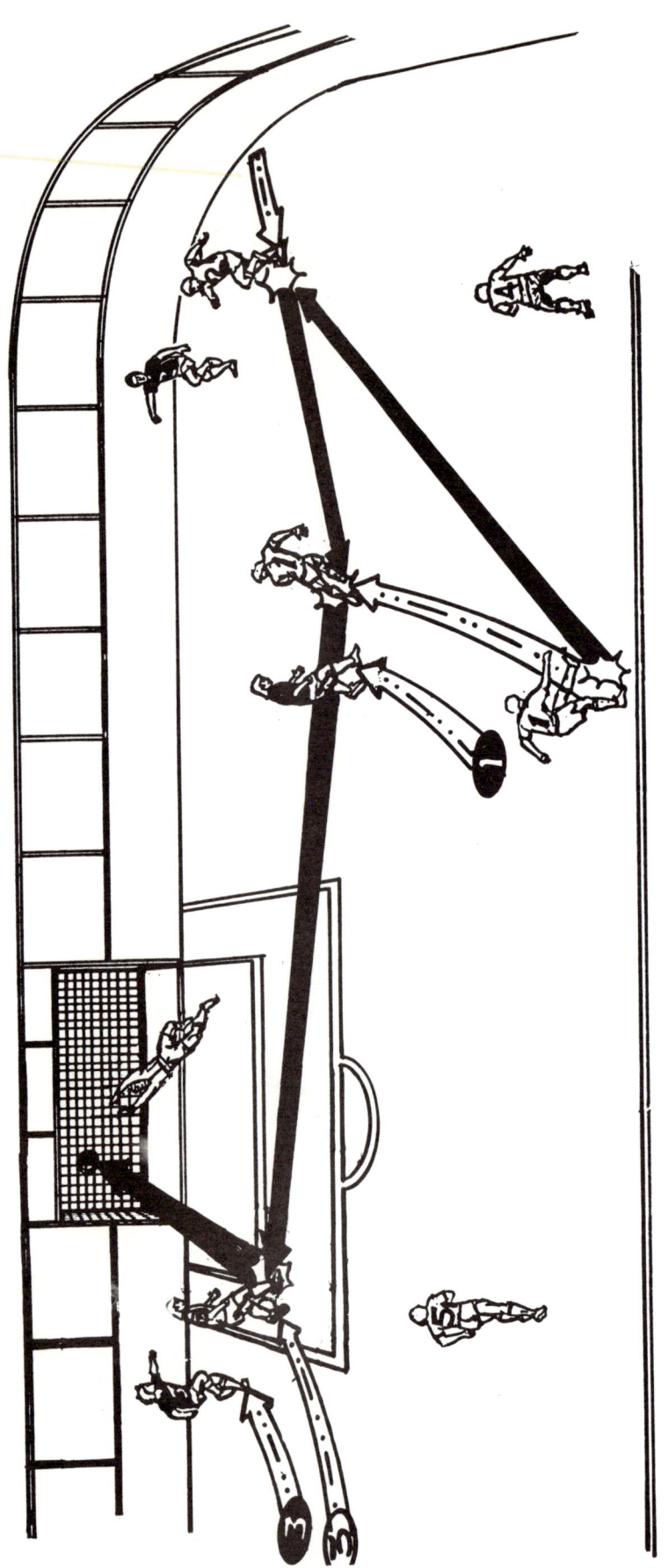

Set Play From The Red Line (Fig. 67)

(a) White #1 plays a one-two with White #2.
(b) He then plays the return pass first time to White #3, who shoots.
(c) White #4 and #5 balance the attacking formation, and become alternate receivers, if the defenders' positioning prevents the execution of the primary play.

If during the running of any set plays, the play doesn't develop properly, the runners should keep running and rotate back near to their original positions, so that team positional balance is retained.

THE POWER PLAY 6 against 5.

For certain specified fouls or misbehavior, the referee may send a player off the field and into the penalty box. For a designated time (ususally two minutes) his teammates will be playing with one less player than their opponents.

You've got to be able to punish opponents for two minute violations. Quick, first time passing combinations are the way to open holes in the defense for shots that must be taken without hesitation. The possible combinations are numberless, and practice will make them work.

If quick, first time passes and shots are perfected, there's no way four defenders can hold off five determined attackers for two minutes. Several of these combinations should be available to the attackers through **diligent, detailed practice.** You've got to make opponents pay for flagrant, sometimes dangerous fouls.

The attackers have to avoid a feeling of complacency, because of their man advantage. They can't rest a bit at this time. If they are relentless in the search for an opening, the chance of scoring is high. Sooner or later the defenders will make a mistake. After all, they are faced with a situation where every movement of the ball forces one of them to try to mark two men at once.

You've been trying to create spare man opportunities all night, and here it's guaranteed to you for two minutes. Be prepared to take full advantage of it.

Similar first time tactics should be used in the sixth attacker situation.

The Power Play: Six Against Five (Fig. 68)

(a) Quick, first time passes penetrate the four man defense and score.
(b) The well timed run of White #1 puts him in position to deflect the ball first time into goal.

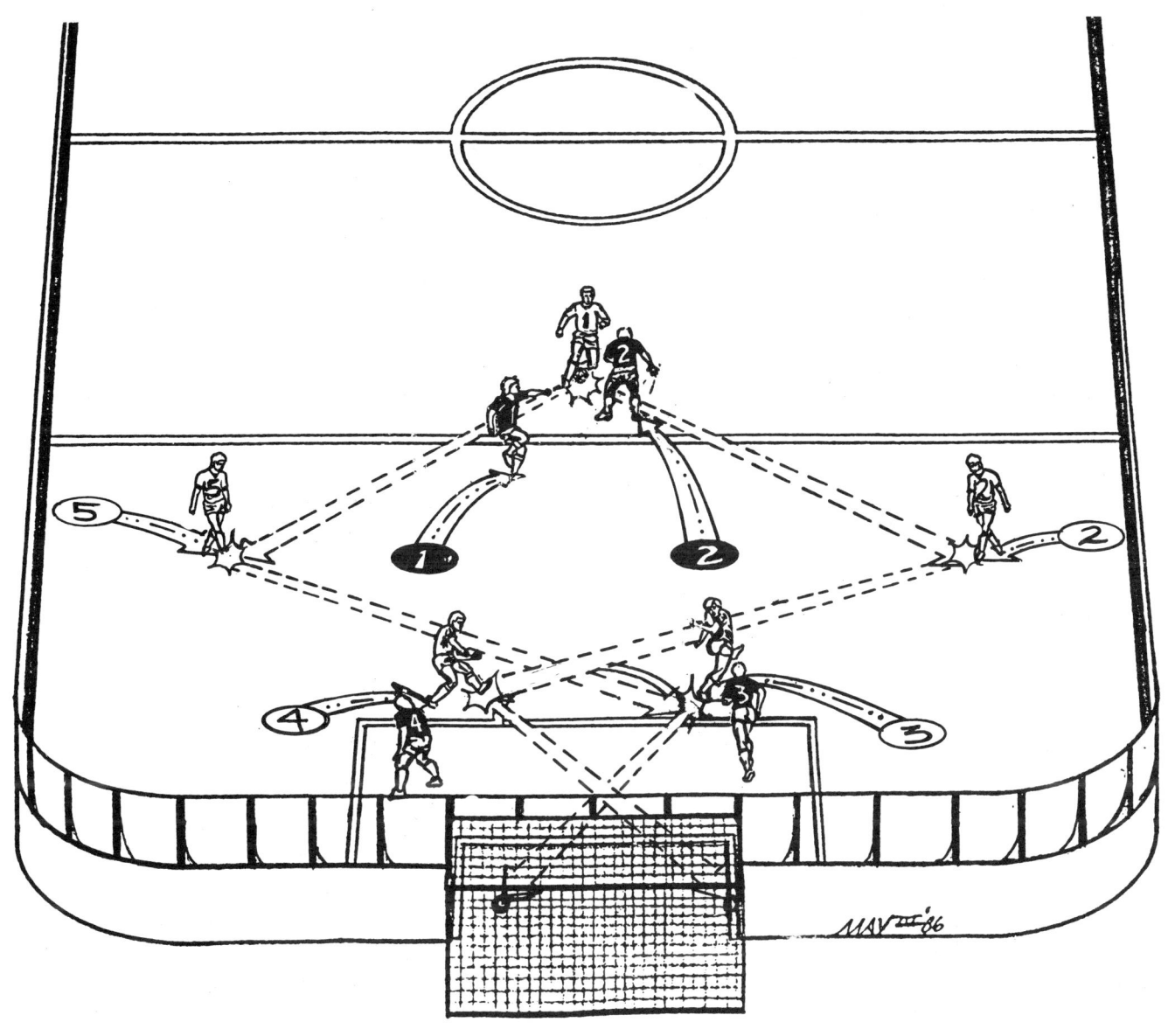

The Power Play: 6 Against 5 (Fig. 69)

(a) Black #4 and Black #3 match up with White #4 and White #3.
(b) Black #1 and #2 try to contain the three top players White #1, #2, and #5.
(c) If Black #1 closes down on the ball, the play goes White #1 to White #5 to White #3 for the shot.
(d) If Black #2 closes down on the ball, the play goes White #1 to White #2 to White #4 for the shot.
(e) All passes are first time passes if possible.

DEFENSIVE PLAY

Professional coaches agree that any system of play begins with a good understanding of defensive responsibilities.

Roy Turner, head coach of the **Wichita Wings** in the **Major Indoor Scocer League says,** "I think everybody has to be totally honest defensively. I think people have got to take responsibility defensively, because everybody in the indoor game has to go both ways. Most people who play soccer like to go forward. Not everyone likes to defend. With the champions and winners, the bottom line comes when everybody is so honest defensively, the same as they would like to feel they have been on offense."

In a game we often leave the defensive duties to each other. We don't react soon enough to defensive requirements, expecting the man next to us to make the tackle or other move.

This is wrong, and if it happens, the attacking team will find the weak spot and exploit it. Honest defense means disciplining ourselves to the point that we respond instantly to the defensive requirements of the game, so that as a team we regain possession of the ball as soon as possible. Without the ball we can't win. We can't even have fun. Defensive honesty is the first requirement, shouldering our fair share of the defensive load.

If you were suddenly aware that your house was on fire, you would rush to check certain areas. Have the kids gotten out? Where are the pets? Can I get to my valuables? etc.

This is the urgency needed for the transition from attack to defense, whenever you lose the ball. You have immediate priorities as a team and as individuals.

The man nearest the ball has to close down on it and slow the ball carrier's progress. Every other player must close down and tightly mark the opponent nearest himself. From here, by hard work, you can make it very difficult for the other team to play, and you'll get the ball back.

From the Pro's: **Ken Cooper** Head Coach of the **Baltimore Blast**
"When we lose the ball, we try to cut down the passing lanes. We like to pressure the ball, and then we like to "sag in", which is a basketball principle."
"The nearest man to the ball pressures the ball, everybody else sags in and cuts down the passing lanes."
As you funnel back toward your defensive zone, each player should be poised to tackle should the man on the ball make an error, or to intercept should he try to pass off.
By shifting around as the attackers pass the ball around, the defenders present a shield against any possible passes or shots, and a supporting defense should the ball carrier attack with a dribble.

Quick movement in adjusting to the changing positions of the ball is the key to a tight defense. If you stand around, you're finished.

You'll be playing a combination of man to man and zone. Watch your man very closely, but be ready to turn him over to a teammate and shift to another man if the movement of the attack demands it.

You need communication to defend properly. Listen for calls from your keeper and other teammates, so you can adjust to whatever movement the attackers throw at you.

When you are one on one against the man on the ball think of when you were a kid and you used to get in peoples way just as a fun way to annoy them. Do the same here. Stay in the guy's way. There's no secret to it. Just stay in front of him until he makes a mistake or is forced to pass. By keeping your knees well bent and taking short quick steps, you can prevent him from getting by you. Patience and restraint are the key words here.

THE ZONE DEFENSE

A zone defense sets up to cover the defensive areas to the best advantage possible. It shifts with the changing positions of the ball to present a curtain of legs and bodies as a shield against any shots, and a deterrent to any passes. As the attackers pass the ball around looking for an opening, the defender nearest the ball moves to close down and pressure the player with the ball.

Through verbal and visual communications with each other, the defenders decide when to stay with the man on the ball, and when to turn him over to the next defender as the man on the ball moves into another zone.

MAN FOR MAN DEFENSE

Man for man coverage means that all defensive players pick an attacker to mark as the defense sets up. You stay tight with your man until the completion of the attacking maneuver.

However, the constantly shifting movements of the attack will catch the defenders out of position at times, making it necessary to hand attacking players over to each other. When this happens, you have a partial zone defense, because to try to keep marking a man who has beaten you can lead to disaster. Your teammates have to shift, and one of them has to leave his man to cover your mistakes.

In the close quarters of indoor soccer, most defenses become a zone plus partial man to man marking, because it's harder to penetrate either dribbling or passing.

Occasionally a sudden tackle attempt will be succesful by the man nearest the ball, giving him a good chance for a scoring shot. Usually this won't be possible, and a delaying strategy is best. An attempt should be made to shuttle play to the side, away from the middle. Try to force any shots to be made from a bad angle. If you allow the play to come down the middle, any shots taken will have a much larger goal area to enter and score.

Now the attacker with the ball is faced with a tough problem. With his teammates tightly marked, it will be hard to complete a pass to them. He will have to try to beat his man with a dribble. His defender should herd him to the side and give ground, watching for a mistake so he can tackle the ball.

If the attacker should beat his man with a dribble, the defender should pursue him immediately. Even if he doesn't catch him, he will force him to play the ball quicker than he wants to, and cut down his space to maneuver. If the defender gives up and doesn't pursue his man, the defense ends up outnumbered by one man and in a very dangerous situation.

As play moves toward the goal, space becomes tighter and tighter, presenting the attacking team with a problem in moving on the goal. Sooner or later the attacking team will have to shoot the ball, but by now there are a lot of players in the way, both attackers and defenders. When a shot is made, every possible attempt should be made to block it. Good defensive teams block many shots before they ever get through to the goal keeper. Closing down on the man with the ball and blocking his shot should be a part of every teams training sessions.

As a team you have to establish yourself defensively before you can go forward with composure and organization. Good defense needs mutual confidence betweeen keeper and defenders. If the defenders leave themselves outnumbered and allow wide open shots to be taken at their goal, the keeper becomes shell shocked and loses his compusure. If the keeper lets stoppable shots go in, the defenders let up on their efforts.

Make opponents earn their goals. Play sound basic defense. Get back in time on the transition. Show the determination that good defense requires. If you lose, let it be because of superior opposition. Don't beat yourself. If you're having an off day, play tough defense and see to it that your opponents don't have an easy day.

Remember, you dominate other teams with tenacious and tough tackling. Defense dominates a game by giving you more possession time, and by mentally frustrating and intimidating the opposition by not giving them room to play.

Encourage your teammates during play. Negative criticism won't transmit any skill to them, but enthusiastic encouragement by showing you support and appreciate their efforts will often help them play beyond their normal ability.

DEFENSIVE TIPS

From the Pro's: Tips on playing defense
Steve McLean, Defender for the **Wichita Wings** of the **MISL**

Question: "How do you defend against the ricochet ball played against the boards. Do you watch the ball or the man?"

Answer: "You have to see both. You have to know where the player is and you have to have an understanding of how the ball is going to come off the boards, where it's going to eventually come to, and also have an eye on your man, to see both. When the ball comes off the boards you try to change it's direction. Instead of trying to bring it down in that kind of situation, it's just a deflection to throw the forward off balance."

"He's already timed it, he knows how it's coming off the boards, he wants to hit it, and if you just get a deflection, it throws him totally off. Then you can turn and recover from there. Prior to the game, as a defender, I'll have someone play some balls in, to see how they're going to ricochet different ways."

Question: "Is there any particular advice you would give to defenders?"

Answer: "Always try to stay on your feet. Never leave your feet unless it's absolutely necessary. Never jump into tackles, you get burned very easily that way. A good forward loves someone who comes in that way. It's best to keep your feet. Let the forward try to jink you one way or the other, then when the time is right, close him down and put in the tackle."

"You also have to work on your going forward skills, because you get some forwards who don't like to mark up. They don't like to track you. If you do a lot of running going forward, I think that it's good to work on your dribbling skills and your one touch passing. You're going to come into play a lot of times under pressure situations at the back. You're going to need that one touch skill and good vision, of always knowing where your teammates are and be able to get the ball to them without having to bring it down first."

"Practice with a partner, or even against a wall. Just play one time passes from different distances and angles."

To Head Coach **Willy Roy** of the **Chicago Sting** of the **MISL**.

Question: "Since so many goals are scored from ricochets, balls played off the boards, how do you coach your defenders to handle that ricochet shot?"

Answer: "You can't stop the shot off the boards, but what you look for is the players running in to follow up the play, that might be running in looking at the rebound coming off the boards. That's the guy you've got to pick up and make sure he doesn't get an easy header or shot off the rebound. The defender has to both watch the ball and know where his attacker is."

Question: "What's the most glaring error a team makes that allows goals to be scored?"

Answer: "There are several of them. You have to close down your offensive players immediately in front of goal. You can't give them any point blank shots on goal."

"The other thing is ball watching. If you are in a situation where someone does shoot off the boards and you're watching only the ball, the attacker runs behind your back and has an open tap-in. So that's the mental part of the game."

To **Tiemo Liekoski**, Head Coach of the **Clevend Force** of the **MISL**.

Question: "From the coaching standpoint, what's the most difficult message to get across to the players about the game?"

Answer: "I think the fact that you have to play man to man, and you have to work hard all the time indoors. You can't really hide at all, and I think we are starting to learn that. In the outdoor game you can hide a little, but in the game we play, there's no place to hide, because you get exposed as soon as you take a holiday on the field."

DEFENSIVE ERRORS

To **Bob McNab**

Question: "What are some glaring errors, commonly made, that allow goals to score?"

Answer: "I think there are two things really. One I would call ball watching. That is watching the ball when it's in another area of the field and allowing the man you are marking to slip behind you, or slip away from you, or pull off you into a much more advantageous position. That's what's known as ball watching, and it's a cardinal sin."

"The other one, I think defending players get too tight up. They're so anxious when the ball gets close to their goal that they get too tight and they get rolled, they get turned, and they get to stand up straight. They should crouch down so they can see the ball. They should maintain at least an arm's length distance from their man even in front of goal. I like aggressive play. I like aggressive defense. I like aggressive offense. I always emphasize that we're only defending because we have to, and we want to get that ball back as quick as we can. And if we can get it back in their half, we're going to do so, because then there are less defenders to get to their goal."

To **Neill Roberts**: Defender for the **Chicago Sting** of the**MISL**.

Question: "As a defender, what's the hardest part of the game for you?"

Answer: "The forwards are always moving around the box, and you have to watch the people who are coming forward with the ball, and you have to keep your eye on the man you should be marking. It's very difficult, because you've got to watch the ball and the man, and the forwards are switching all the time, so you've got to be very aware in the box, you've got to always be looking around you, and you know when you've got good players coming into you with the ball, and intelligent forwards sweeping around behind, it makes it very, very difficult. In such a confined space as indoor is, there are a lot of shots and a lot of goals."

THE FULL COURT PRESS

Pressuring the ball and sagging back is one way to defend. Another way is to apply strong pressure all over the floor while the ball is deep in your opponents defensive zone. This is especially effective against a goal keeper who can't play the ball well with his feet.

If you pressure the two back players and mark tight on all the rest, the back players will have to play the ball to their keeper. If the keeper is good with his feet, he will first dribble the ball up field and pass the ball among his back players until the ball has been moved out of his defensive end. No problem. By moving out of his goal and up field he becomes the spare man, making sure there is always an open man to whom to pass. (see diagrams 46 & 47.)

If he's not confident of his foot skills, he'll probably play a long ball up field to relieve the pressure. The defending team will be looking for this, and will be positioned in the best way for an interception. A ball that's played long and in the air gives the defenders the most time to get to it and intercept.

If the goal keeper is under circumstances where he has to play the ball with his feet, he can sometimes be trapped and tackled when the ball is passed to him. This can happen when he has already played the ball once from his hands, or if he is outside the penalty area.

The two defending players pressuring the attacking back players watch for the pass to the keeper. When it's made, the nearest man quickly closes down the keeper and tries to tackle the ball. If he's successful, he has a tap in for a goal, If he's not, he lets his team open for a counter attack, because the keeper passes to the man left open. (see diagram #46) If this happens, the defender has to chase back to prevent uneven numbers.

Back players under pressure are more likely to play a long ball forward than to take on a man deep in their defensive zone. The full court press is intended to apply sudden pressure on a team in their own defensive area, so that they misplay a short pass or attempt a long pass that can be cut off.

The full court press is very tiring, because of the intensity of effort needed to make it succeed. Take this into consideration when using the tactic, so that you make frequent substitutions.

Full court pressure can unsettle your opponents, and cause turnovers of the ball. It can be a very useful defensive weapon if your entire team understands how to use it.

From the Pro's: **Mark Peterson:** Forward, **Tacoma Stars** of the**MISL.**

"Anytime you put someone under pressure, it makes it a lot harder for him to play no matter how good he is."

Question: "It's a lot of work though isn't it?"

Answer: "Yes it is, but I think if you really analyze it, if you put them under pressure **early** and **everybody** does it, it's less work. That's the key, **everybody** has to do it. If one person doesn't do it, they just pass the ball to that guy and he's free."

"If everybody does it I think it's less running in the end than if you drop back. If you pressure early, you might win the ball back and get a strike on goal right away."

Sometimes in defending, you can invite the pass to be made to your man by appearing to lose track of his position. Give the passer the notion he has space to make the pass, but be ready to close down and intercept. Many subtleties of movement go on, and much feinting and faking by both attackers and defenders. It's cat and mouse and you aim to come out on top.

Defensive Full Court Pressure (Fig. 70)

(a) Black players #2, #3, #4 and #5 move up almost alongside and tight to their men to be in a position to intercept any passes.

(b) Under pressure from Black #1, White #1 passes to his goal keeper.

(c) Black #1 quickly closes down the keeper, tackles the ball, and taps it into the net.

Fig. 70

DEFENDING AGAINST THE ONE-TWO or WALL PASS

Defenders must learn to deal with the wall pass or the one-two. The reason the one-two works so well is because the defender is caught facing one way while the attackers are facing the other way. In other words the attackers are already facing the direction the ball is moving.

The defender closing down on the man with the ball must always be ready to turn quickly when his man plays the ball off, because the ball will be coming back instantly.

What usually happens is the defender is so intent on closing down his man tightly, that he forgets to be ready to turn and go with him to prevent the one-two pass.

By varying his defensive movement, the defender can help to throw off the attackers timing. In other words, keep moving while you mark your man. Move in tight, then move back a little, then move slightly to one side then to the other.

Defending Against The One-Two (Fig. 71)

(a) White #1 dribbles froward, and commits Black #1 to challenge.

(b) White #1 then passes to White #2, and dashes by to receive the return pass.

(c) But, Black #1 is alert to the move, pivots quickly, and drops back to intercept the pass.

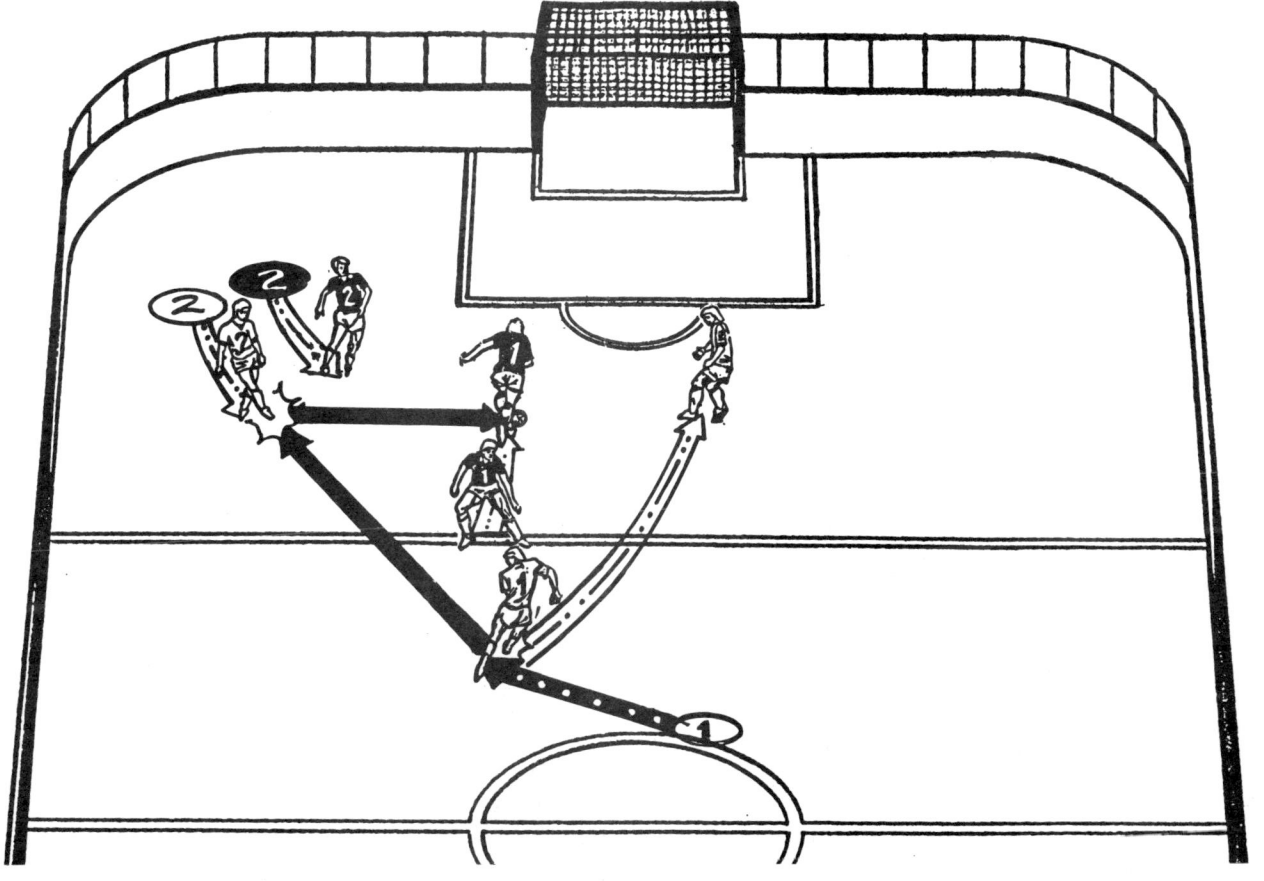

Fig. 71

By being unpredictable and always ready to turn with your man, and always mentally alert to the things the attackers may do, you can learn to cope with the one-two pass. In fact you have to. If you allow the attackers to consistently play wall passes against you, you are in for a long and frustrating evening.

During this defensive play, a lot of talking should be going on among the defenders. The attackers will be changing positions constantly, and the defenders will be constantly turning over their man to other defenders and picking up other men as the priorities keep changing.

Players should make every effort to make their calls helpful and instructive. Players can also communicate by pointing as well as talking. For instance a player might shout "pick him up" and point to a man at the same time.

DEFENSIVE BODY POSITION (Fig. 72)

In defense, when you are jockeying and containing a player with the ball as you give ground, take up the following position:

Knees should be well bent; feet close enough together so he can't push the ball between your legs, but wide enough apart so that you can move sideways easily; **full** surface of the soles of your feet in contact with the floor; weight centered right over the ankles for balance.

Try to maintain this body position as you retreat, slowing him down as much as possible. This position, with the knees well bent while you're **relaxed** yet alert, will allow you to shadow his every movement and keep him from getting past you.

If you are faster than he is, you can close down tight on him. If he is faster than you, you have to give him a little more room. All the time you should watch his **solar plexus** while seeing the ball with your peripheral vision. (The solar plexus is a spot about the size of a baseball about two inches above the navel.) It's the center of balance, the center of effort. All movement emanates from it. No matter how your opponent twists and turns, his solar plexus tells where he is really going. He can't fake with that area. Wherever it goes, he goes. Practice this defensive containment frequently, using a friend or teammate for an opponent. You have to be able to slow him down, and then pounce firmly into the tackle when he makes a mistake.

Fig. 72

ONE ON ONE TACKLING (Fig. 73)

Sometimes in open field situations, when you have no cover from your teammates, it is dangerous to attempt a tackle on a skillful ball handler. If you miss, he has a clear path to goal. It's better to close down on him and shuttle him toward the sideboards waiting for back-up help. Then put in the tackle or force the pass. The illustration shows the tactics involved.

Fig. 73

DOUBLE TEAMING ON DEFENSE (Fig. 74)

It's difficult to take the ball away from a really good dribbler as we all know. One way is to double team him as in basketball. All players should **mark tight** off the ball, and the defender facing the man with the ball should attempt to maneuver him toward the side boards and toward one of his teammates, so that at just the right time his teammate can pounce in to help with the tackle.

This teammate has to leave the man he has been marking, but if his move is sudden and unexpected the defense should end up with the ball. Even if the move doesn't succeed the defenders can usually recover their positioning because of the tight space involved.

As with every strategy, the **time** and the **place** are all important. Remember this is a thinking game, or should be. Practice, practice, practice until thought becomes instantaneous action. It's a game that gives back whatever you put into it. This applies to players both male and female and to any age group.

Fig. 74

Double Teaming On Defense (Fig. 74)

    (a) Black #1 shuttles the attacker White #1 to the sideboards.
    (b) Black #2 moves in to help with the tackle.
    (c) Black #3 shifts to mark White #2.
    (d) Black #5 shifts to mark White #3.
    (e) Black #4 is ready to cover the area where the ball might come out.
    (f) White #5 is left unmarked, but he's furthest from the ball, and the passing lanes to him are cut off.

DEFENDING AGAINST CROSSING PASSES OR CORNER KICKS (Fig. 75)

In most marking, the defender stays **goalside** of the man he is marking. This is to prevent the man from getting behind him. In indoor soccer it is sometimes safe to cheat a little on this by moving up so you are alongside but still somewhat behind him. This will give you a getter chance of intercepting the pass.

Close in front of the goal you can't afford to stand behind your man, especially if the ball is being crossed from the side as in a corner kick.

If a ball is played from the side across the goal mouth, the player who gets the first touch on it is the one who wins that confrontation. If it's an attacking player, his chances of deflecting it first time into goal are very good. As a defender you must get to the ball first. That is your top priority.

To do this you have to be positioned alongside him and slightly goalside or in front of him and slightly goalside (see Fig. 75).

On set plays such as corner kicks and inbounds passes, the attackers will be making all sorts of runs to free themselves to receive passes. The defenders must move with them, always retaining positions from which they can get to the ball first, when it is played in and across goal.

The most useful tool a defender has are his eyes. He has to know what is going on in front of him and in back. His head must swivel to take in the action from all points.

You need to know where the ball is and what's going on behind you at all times. Even experienced players can be guilty of ball "watching", and become so engrossed in watching the play around the ball that they let attackers creep in behind them with disasterous results.

Use your head and eyes and listen to the calls from your goalkeeper to keep fully aware of what is happening behind you.

Defending Against Crossing Passes And Corner Kicks (Fig. 75)

(a) White #1 plays in the pass toward White #2.

(b) Black #2 by correct positioning is able to get to the ball first..

On crossing balls, the defenders have all marked so that they are in front of the attackers **in relation to the ball.** In this way they are in a position to get to the ball first and cut off any passes. Attackers should try to get clear by intelligent, well timed runs.

Fig. 75

DEFENDING AGAINST THE COUNTER ATTACK

When facing a counter attack, the defenders will often find themselves outnumbered. Delay is the strategy here.

If it's 2 on 1, or 3 on 2, the outnumbered defenders have to delay the action until their teammates can recover and fall back to help.

The defenders can't close down tight on the attackers or they will be beaten by a pass to the open man.

With 2 on 1 the defender closes down half way between the two attackers and goalside of them so that the man on the ball hesitates between keeping it and passing it off. This slows the attack down a little and should give his teammates the chance to hurry back to help. (see counter attack drills, pages 85, 86, 87.

The defender faced with two men has to feint first toward one attacker and then toward the other as he retreats, to keep them guessing what he is going to do. He has to give the outside man more room than the man in the middle to try to force any shot to be made from the outside which will give the shooter a poorer angle than from straight in front of goal.

As the play nears the goal and the defender forces the ball to be passed to the outside man, the goal keeper has to be ready either to block the shot from the outside or to come out and intercept the pass coming across to the attacker coming down the middle.

Feinting and faking by the defender and the keeper can sometimes make the attackers hesitate just enough to lose their advantage.

DEFENDING AGAINST THE POWER PLAY

In a man-short defense, four defenders face five attackers. A shifting zone defense is the usual answer to this situation.

You will have to vary your defensive formation to match the attacking formation you are facing. If the attackers station one man in front of goal, you'll probably use a diamond defense. If the attackers station two men in front of goal, you'll probably use a box defense. Experimentation will lead you to the best man-short defense for your team.

From the Pro's **Bob McNab** former head coach of the **Tacoma Stars** of the **MISL** on defensive tactics playing a man short against the power play.

"Basically in essence there are two systems of play, well three. **Diamond** or **box** or you can have one at the front and three at the back. We tend to play box. We also try to show them diamond, so that they'll set up differently. What you're really doing, you're taking the **positive space,** the valuable space, and giving them what I woud describe as the **negative space** 'round the sides."

"You want them to play around you, rather than let them penetrate. You want to make them pass the ball. You want to pressure them, and what you want to do is take away the lanes. **You take away the passing lanes."**

"When you pressure the ball, if you come in from a certain angle, you can eliminate their spare player. If I come to one side of you, you can't pass the ball through me. They've got to work very, very hard then, either by dribbling or passing movements so they can get the ball to their spare man on the opposite side of the field. And you always leave the man furthest from the ball free. You mark the strong side and leave them the weak side. It's similar principles to basketball."

Rick Benben: Head coach of the **Kansas City Comets** of the **MISL** favors a different approach against the power play.

Question: "When you're playing a man short, what is the method you generally use?"

Answer: "The method we use is one where we help the goal keeper protect the goal. We use our two defenders to stay with the goal keeper and help block shots. They match up man to man with the attackers closest to the goal. Then our two players up on top try to do the best they can in covering the three players around the top. We don't worry very much about pressure on the other team. We try to absorb a lot of pressure."

Defending Against The Power Play: The Box Formation (Fig. 76)

Illustrations "A" and "B" are sequences of the same play. They show the movement of the four defenders as the ball changes position. Play "B" is a continuation of Play "A".

Play "A"
(a) With White #1 in possession, Black #4 would be marking him.
(b) Black #1 would be marking White #2.
(c) When the ball is passed to the right to White #5, Black #4 has to slide across and mark White #5.
(d) Black #1 would move across to White #1.
(e) That gives us strong side marking, with White #2 becoming the spare man furthest from the ball. The passing lanes to him are cut off.

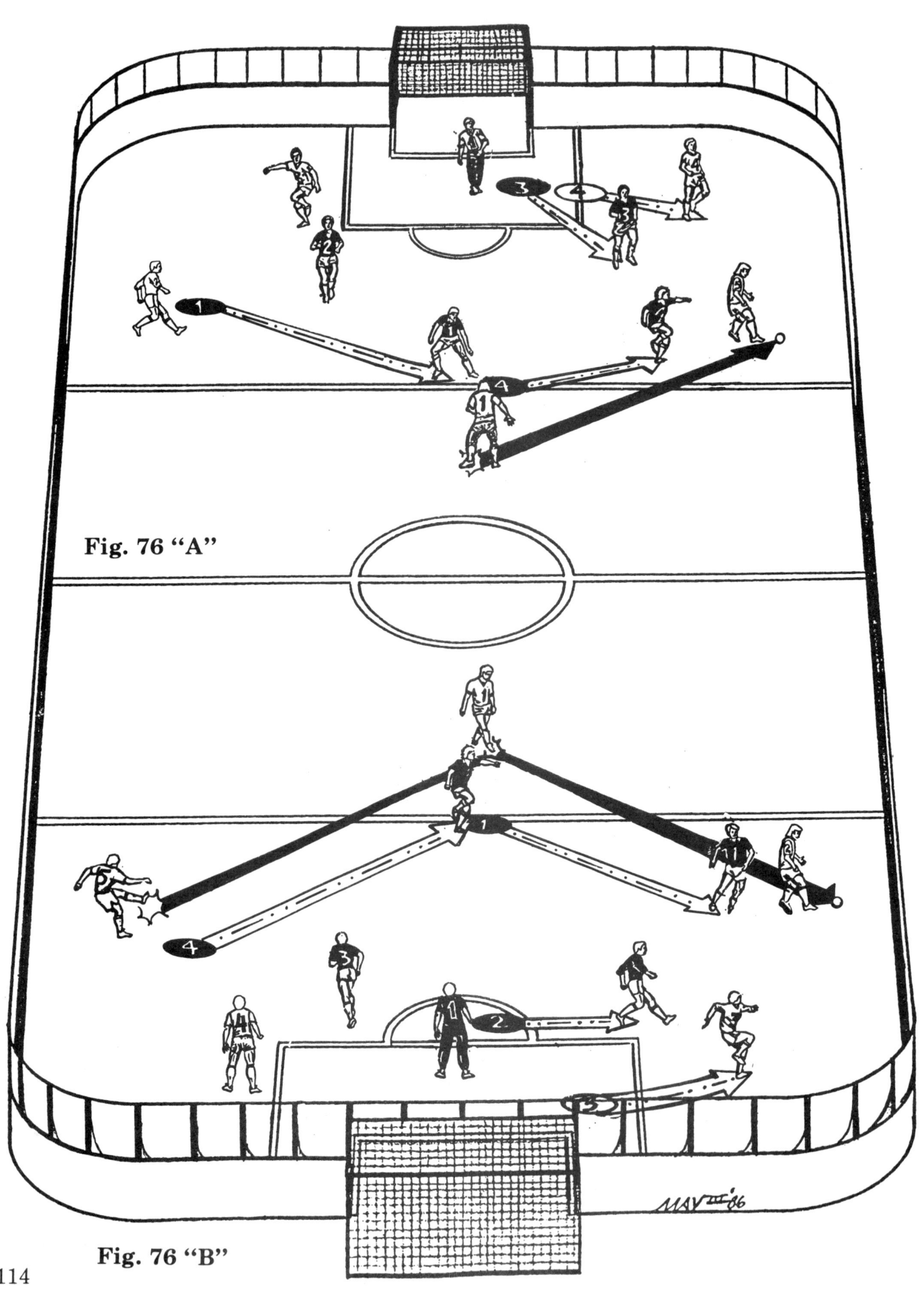

Fig. 76 "A"

Fig. 76 "B"

Play "B"

(a) White #5 plays the ball back to White #1 who then passes to the left side to White #2.
(b) Black #1 slides across to mark White #2.
(c) Black #4 moves to mark White #1.
(d) This leaves White #5 as the spare man furthest from the ball.

In this manner, the four defenders try to force the attackers to play around the perimeter, rather than be able to penetrate. The two front defenders, Black #1 and #4, have to be very active, since they have three attackers to contend with. The movements won't be exactly as shown, because the attackers are constantly on the move probing for an opening. These two illustrations show the basic principles behind the box defense.

Defending Against The Power Play: The Diamond Formation (Fig. 77)

Play "B" is a continuation of Play "A"

Play "A"

(a) White #1 passes to White #2.
(b) Black #1 moves over to mark White #2.
(c) White #4 moves across to the far post.
(d) White #1 is left as the spare man.

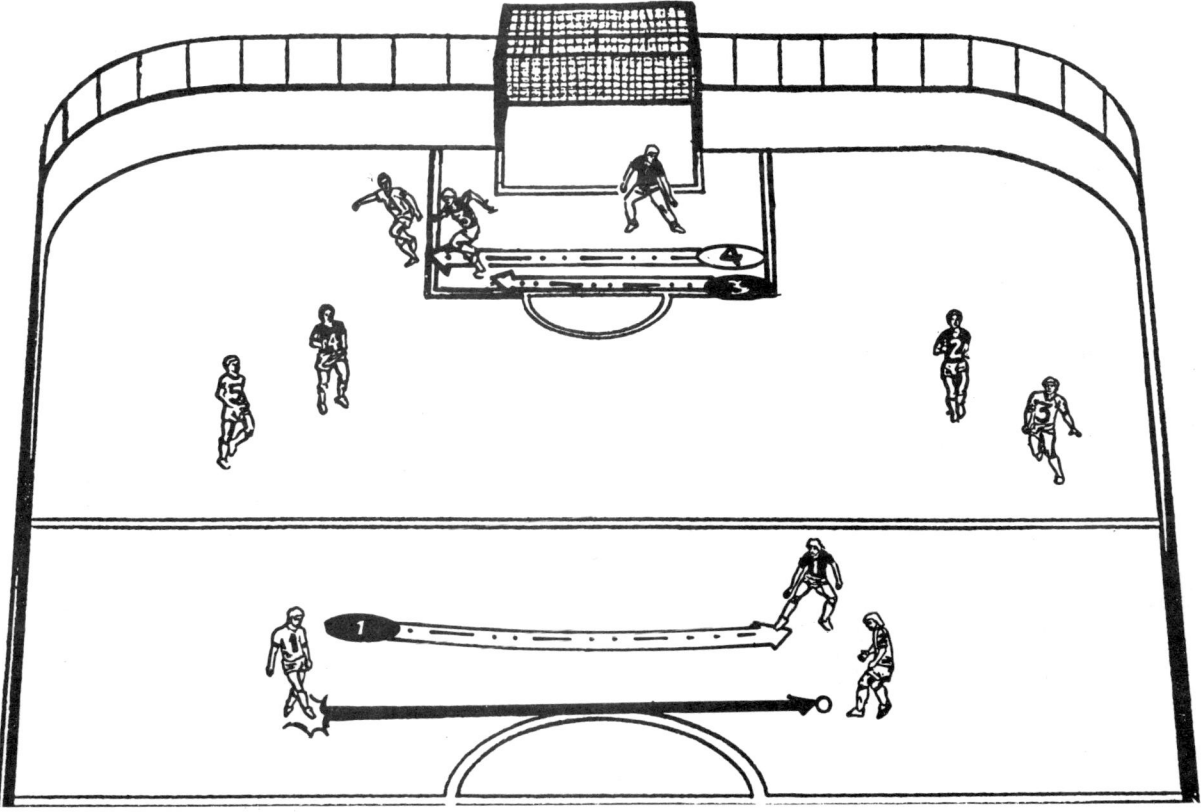

Fig. 77 "A"

Play "B"

(a) White #2 passes back to White #1.
(b) Black #2 switches over to mark White #1.
(c) White #4 moves across to the far post.
(d) White #2 becomes the spare man.

The diamond formation would be used when the attackers put one man in by the goal, and two men out on top. The defenders match up with the man in front of goal and the two men out at the sides. This leaves the one defender left to do the best he can to mark the two attackers on top. He has to chase back and forth with the movement of the ball.

This is an approximation of how the diamond formation is set up. The movement of the attackers will call for various adjustments as play progresses.

Fig. 77 "B"

THE GOAL KEEPER IN DEFENSE

Stopping shots on goal is of first importance to the goal keeper. A really good shot stopper can keep you in the game, even when you are being outplayed in the field.

We have all seen a match in which the keeper just couldn't be beaten. All good keepers have a game like this now and then. I don't think anyone knows why this happens, least of all the goal keeper himself. His reflexes are perfect; he reads the angles just right; and his confidence is supreme. Of course he is drawing on all those long, grueling hours of painful practice that are now paying him back in full measure.

I think the best way to learn these techniques and secrets is to study the moves of good keepers, and to pick their brains at every opportunity. Never be too shy or too proud to ask for help. Most accomplished and talented people are extremely helpful if they are asked for advice. If you have a thirst for knowledge, you can find it.

From the Pro's: **Chris Vaccaro,** Goal keeper for the **Cleveland Force** of the **MISL.**

Question: "Which type of shot is the most difficult to handle?"

Answer: "I think the ball that is played off the boards and ricochets off the boards to the middle is the most dangerous shot. And the other most dangerous shot is when you're screened, when you have several players in front of you and it's tough to see the ball. You have to get into a different position, and sometimes it's out of position. The action is so fast that I have to maybe take a half step or a step over, and get myself actually out of position for the shot, to react to the shot. Otherwise if I can't see it, I'm in bigger trouble than if I can see it. If I can't see the foot hit the ball, it might be too late, before I can react to the ball."

Advice to goal keepers: "In the indoor game you just want to work a lot on the boards and a lot of reaction drills and reflex drills and quickness drills."

"Work on quickness and getting down, getting down as quick as you can, and getting up quickly. Just **reacting** to the shot and **not trying to guess or go down too soon.** It's better to stay on your feet and use your reflexes to your best advantage. If there is a deflexion you're still in a good position to react to another shot. If you go down too early the ball could be deflected into a corner or something."

The basic techniques of stopping shots are the same outdoors or indoors. The biggest difference is the shots come from shorter distances indoors. A compensating factor is the much smaller goal. Some big men seem to fill the entire goal with their body, arms, and legs.

Good vision and coolness under fire are indispensable assets for the keeper. He must remain relaxed yet alert while furious action goes on in front of him. One way that can help him remain composed is to learn to use deep abdominal breathing while the ball is at the other end of the floor. This is done through the nose. The abdominal area goes in and out as you **slowly** inhale and exhale. The chest doesn't enter into it very much. It's all abdominal. It's almost impossible to remain tense when you breathe this way. Try it. Be sure to exhale completely each breath.

COMING OFF THE LINE

One technique that is frequently overlooked is that of coming off the line to block or smother a shot. When an attacker comes in close with a clear chance for an unobstructed shot, the only chance a keeper has is to come off his line to block or smother it.

He has to be quick off his line and go down sideways to block as much area as possible. The suddenness of the move can sometimes freeze the attacker's reactions for an instant, allowing the keeper to reach the ball and block it, or gather it into his hands.

This move takes courage and perfect timing, but when it is mastered it becomes a very valuable tool for the keeper.

He can even come out of the penalty area to block a shot. He may give up a free kick, but that's better than a goal. He must get back to his line immediately, because the free kick may be taken very quickly. Some league rules forbid sliding tackles. If the keeper comes out of the penalty area in a very obvious and intentional manner and leaves his feet to block or handle the ball, he leaves himself open for time in the penalty box.

He should make it look accidental, something that takes place in the urgency of the moment, even though it is a calculated risk he takes to prevent what would be an almost sure goal.

One final word on defense. You can dominate a team with good defense. That means tight marking and determined tackling. If you **work hard** to get the ball, you'll have much more time to **enjoy the fun** of attacking with it.

When you establish your defense, it shows how determined you are, and has that effect on the opposition. If you are half hearted in your defense, the other people can sense it, and they come in for the kill. If you show you really intend to stop them, really defend, then the other teams are affected by it. It takes a little edge off their attack.

SUBSTITUTIONS

Since the team that can maintain it's game at high speed has an advantage, we have to use our substitutions accordingly.

From **Jean Willrich,** midfielder for the **San Diego Sockers** of the **MISL.**

"You must have condition. When you play longer than three minutes in the midfield position, you kill yourself. You fool yourself. You have to give the midfielder a lot of credit, you have to work."

At many amateur games the clock runs continuously. It doesn't stop when the ball is out of play as in the pro's. Consequently the amateur players can probably play three to four minutes a shift. A lot depends on the **intensity** of the play during the shift. Sometimes you will run very little, at other times you can exhaust yourself in a minute and a half. Target men may sometimes stay in longer, because their role doesn't always take quite as much running as say a midfielder. Applying the full court press requires tremendous output, so shifts will be much shorter if you expect to be successful.

Get used to entering the game ready to play at top speed instantly. While you are on the sidelines, keep close attention to what's going on, so you will have your head in the game the moment you step on to the court.

Most amateur players stay in the game too long. Several shifts where you play until you are really tired can exhaust you beyond the point of recovery. This is a mistake, because in the late stages of a tough match you will struggle and be unable to keep up with a team that is still fit and relatively fresh.

The average amateur team should have ten or twelve players to maintain the proper substitution schedule, and keep up the pace that's necessary to win consistently. Desire goes out the window, when you run out of gas.

How you substitute becomes a major tactic indoors. When a player stays in the game too long, his fatigue affects all his reactions. In a scramble for a loose ball in front of goal, if he's tired, he may not get his foot to the ball, and a goal is lost. He may be a little slow in the dribble, and lose the ball. Defensively he may get beat by a man he would normally stop. He gets back a step too late, and the counter attack scores on him. The difference may be slight, but it's often the difference between winning and losing. The team that can maintain it's games at top speed will win. If you just want to play and get tired, and your teammates permit it, stay in as long as you like. **If you want to win,** have at least ten players on your side, and use them properly. Players who stay in the game too long don't understand the tactics of substitution, and the tremendous pace of the indoor game. When you understand how you hurt the team playing tired, you won't need someone to call you out. You'll come out on your own **before** you feel tired. Obey the eleventh commandment, "Thou shalt not kid thyself."

If you stay in the game too long, you have to stay out too long. You cool off, and find yourself out of the game mentally. Late in a game, if a team is too tired to get back on defense soon enough, a good counter attacking team will kill them.

From **Brian Quinn:** All star midfielder for the **San Diego Sockers** of the **MISL.**

"The thing people playing indoor soccer have to realize is the difference between indoor and outdoor soccer. Just recently we played Dynamo Kiev, one of the top rated Russian teams. When they came to play indoor soccer, they found it a lot different. We were taking advantage of them with **quick** changes, good movement off the ball. Last week we played one of the West German clubs, Schalke '04, and they had the same problems. They were obviously good players, great technique, but they tried to change their game from outdoors to indoors and it didn't work, because it's a completely different game. We took advantage of them **staying on the field too long,** their changes weren't quick enough, they were getting tired. They weren't working off the ball quick enough, and they were taking too much time to build up, while we were going quickly."

Question: "Brian, maybe you could mention how long you stay on the floor. My players don't want to come off until they're tired. I want them off before they're tired."

Answer: "I think a good drill to make them realize that is to do a one minute run as fast as they can up and down the field. If they aren't tired after that, then they aren't doing it properly. The maximum time we stay on the field is two minutes, two minutes thirty seconds max."

FORMATIONS OF PLAY

When we speak of formations of play, we are talking about a general "shape" that a team likes to use while playing. It usually reflects the abilities of the players, and the way in which the opponents are playing. Formations are not written in stone. They are **starting places** from which to attack or defend, and they will change their shape as play moves to different areas of the floor.

In all attacking formations, one man will generally stay back a bit to act as a sweeper should the attackers lose the ball. This back man will still be in the attack, but he is prepared for the counterattack should it come. The back man's position will be changing as different attacking runs are made and different men occupy this position by interchanging or rotating.

The biggest differences among the formations occurs in the positioning of the three principle attacking players. If you have two quick forwards and a good passing midfielder, you will probably play 2-1-2. If you have a skilled target man, you will probably play 2-2-1. With a highly talented all 'round attacker, you might play diamond plus one with the striker staying forward for quick counter attacking strikes at goal. As the illustrations show, the defensive formations change their shape as the team moves forward to attack.

These formations are very fluid in practice. They are an attempt to have people where you want them at any given moment. It's still the main business of the attackers to create space to play in by their movement, and the main business of the defenders to deny that space to the attackers.

THE 2-1-2 FORMATION (Two strikers; one midfielder; two defenders) (Fig. 78)

The 2-1-2 is a very balanced formation. It covers the spaces very well. Each player is also in position to cover his teammates if they are beaten by an attacking move.

It's a good attacking formation, because it spreads the defense, and tends to force man to man coverage by the defenders. The ball can be knocked around until an opening comes up for a shot or rebound. Attacker #1 can move around in front of goal looking for a ball off the boards or to play a deflection into goal off a shot by a teammate. He can move further out to play wall passes with other attackers.

THE 2-2-1 FORMATION (Two defenders; Two midfielders; One point man) (Fig. 79)

As a defensive formation, 2-2-1 will usually revert to 2-1-2 since most offenses will send someone down the middle to post up somewhere in front of goal. One of the midfielders would shift to the center to cover this threat, and the striker would move back to patrol the space vacated by the midfielder. This change produces the 2-1-2 defensive formation. Shown by the movement of players #1 and #5.

In attack the 2-2-1 is well suited for a team with a good point man who can receive the ball under pressure with his back to the goal, and feed the ball to midfielders and back men coming through to shoot on goal.

THE DIAMOND PLUS ONE FORMATION (One defender; Two midfielders; Two strikers) (Fig. 80)

In the diamond plus one defense, four players line up in a diamond shape as shown. One player, #2, hangs out near the halfway line, or maybe over it into the attacking half. He's there for a quick outlet pass and counter attack when his team wins the ball. If the attackers commit five players into their attacking half, this #2 defensive player will be completely open if his team collects the ball. On the other hand, his teammates will be defending with four players against five attackers. It's a gambling situation for both teams.

Usually, the attacking team will leave one man back to mark this man, making the numbers even again. It's an interesting and effective way for a defensive team to play, if they have the right players for it. They have to be skilled at the counter attack. It's success also depends a lot on the skill of the advanced player once he receives the ball to beat his man and the goal keeper for a score.

THE NEED FOR TWO WAY PLAYERS

Indoor soccer emphasizes the need for modern day players to be able to play both ways. They have to be good defenders as well as good attackers.

The flow of the game and the quick movements of the ball dictate all players become involved in attack and all players become involved in defense.

The defender who hangs back and only defends will cripple the offensive moves of a team. The attacker who can only attack will destroy a team's defensive cohesion.

Players will still have roughly defined roles as attackers or defenders or midfielders, but for a team to be successful, it must be composed of all around players who are willing to work and perform on all parts of the court in **defense** and **attack.**

When a defender should move up and carry through an attack will come to him with experience and coaching. The same goes for when an attacker should apply defensive play all the way back to his own goal.

Another reason players should work on becoming all 'round performers is the make-up of most amateur teams. They are usually composed of a group of friends with a few strangers recruited to round out the roster. Substitutions are generally made on the basis of who is tired, so the man entering the game may have to take any one of the positions on the field with confidence.

As teams become more familiar with each other, they can quickly adjust positioning during play. Never-the-less, the future belongs to the all around player.

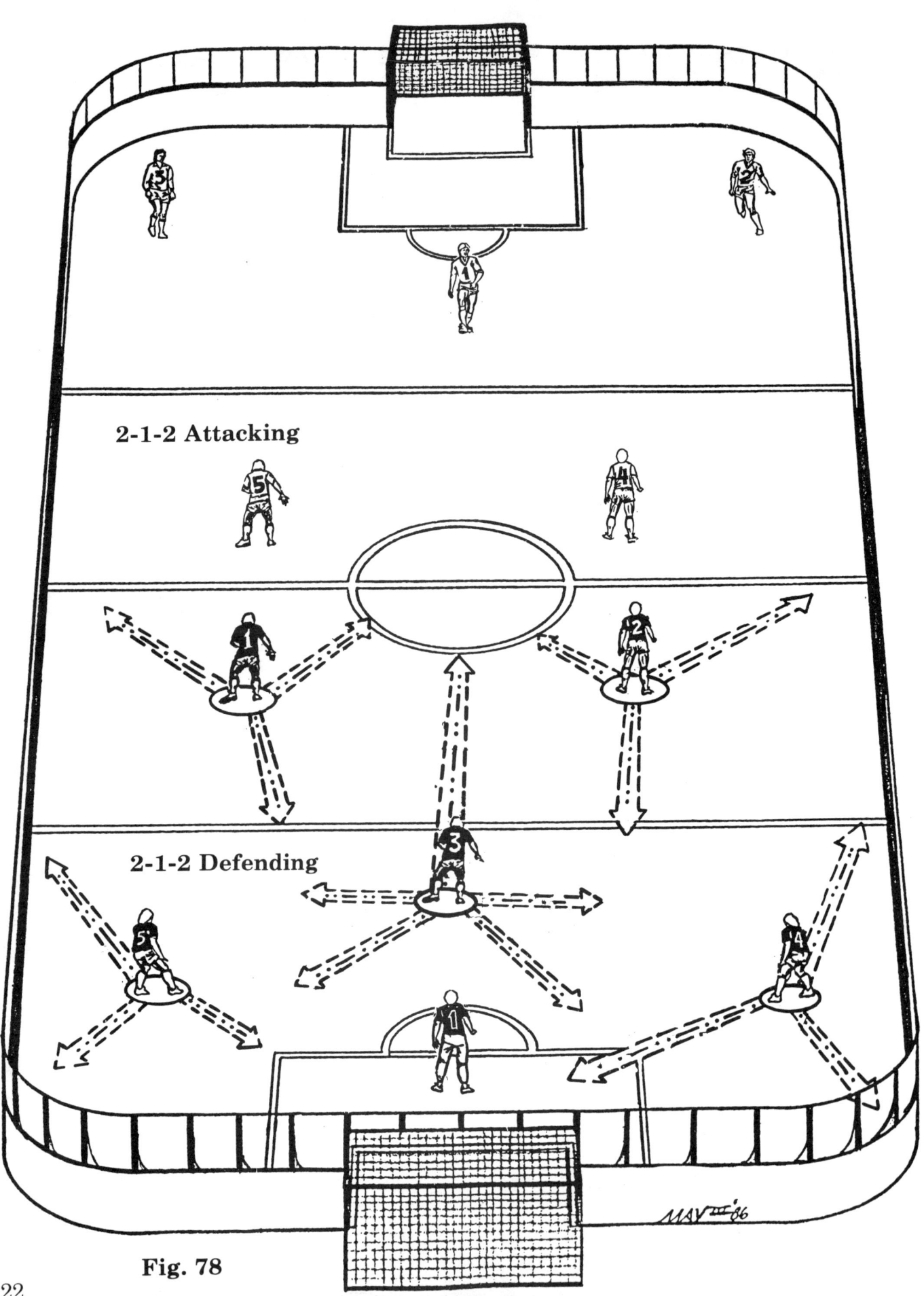

Fig. 78

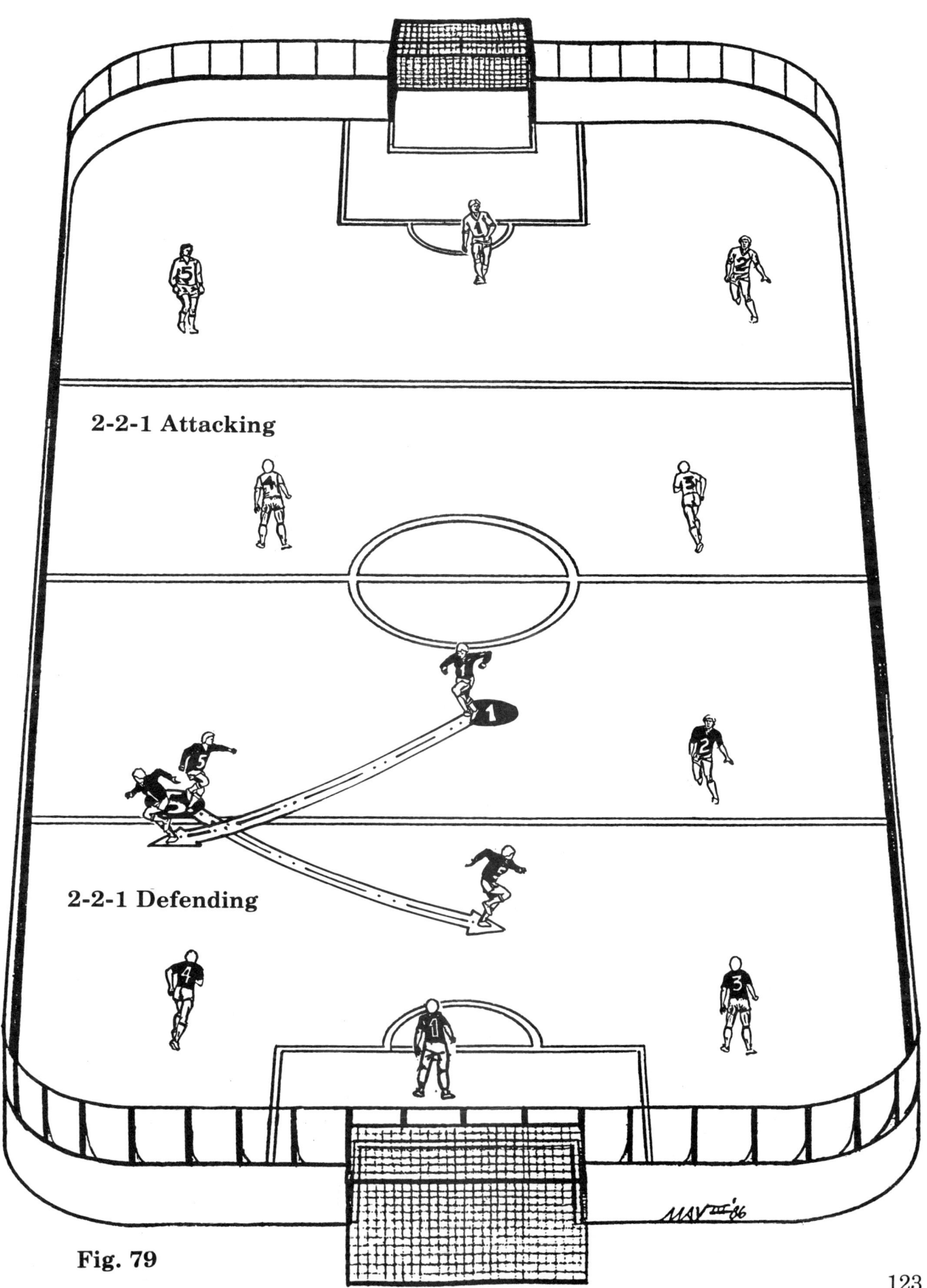

Fig. 79

Diamond Plus One Attacking

Fig. 80

THE REQUIREMENTS OF THE DIFFERENT PLAYER POSITIONS

We have spoken of the need for two way players; people who can attack and defend well, and link up in the middle. It's true that to be successful all players need this all around ability.

Still, each player will have his strong points and consequently will usually be designated as forward, midfielder, or defender, and will take up that position in the basic formations of the team.

The Forward

Anyone playing in the forward position has to score goals. Since he'll spend a great deal of time near the opponents goal, he'll get a lot of opportunities to score, and he must be able to finish these chances with a reasonable degree of regularity.

He has to be quick in starting the counter attack moves, and able to pass the ball well, and be expert in making decoy runs to create space for his teammates. He often has to beat opponents one on one, so dribbling skill is a must. He should spend a lot of practice time with his back to the goal, since that's how he'll be playing a great deal of the time. Defensively he has to mark and chase down the opposing defenders when they make runs with or with out the ball.

The Midfielder

One of the midfielder's primary requirements is stamina. He's involved in nearly every movement of the ball, attacking or defending. Beside this he gets many chances for shots on goal himself. Perhaps his most visible talent is that he seems to be everywhere at once. When an important defensive play is needed, he's there to make it. In the next few seconds he can be found feeding a penetrating pass forward, or shooting on goal.

A good midfielder's ball handling and dribbling skills are flawless, and he seems to play the ball never having to look at it. This vision, this ability to see the entire tactical situation at a glance is another extremely important skill of the midfielder. Lastly, he is a master passer of the ball.

The Defender

Above all, the defender needs a sense of composure, a coolness under fire, that allows him to keep his head under the extreme pressure of being the last barrier to a score. Obviously, his strong points will be tight marking ability, great postional sense, and uncompromising tackling technique. He needs good field vision, and the ability to make helpful calls to teammates playing in front of him. He has great understanding of the people he's playing with, and a sense of leadership that imparts a feeling of steadiness to the team. Lastly, the consumate defender needs good attacking skills, because he often finds himself free to make attacking runs, and to take shots on goal.

THE TOE POKE

Most soccer kicks are made with the inside or outside of the foot, or the full instep.

In close quarters the toe can be used to advantage, because it's quicker and needs less preparation or back lift.

Indoors, lots of goals are scored from very close range in a crowd of players. If you find your close-in shots being blocked because you don't have enough time, try poking the ball with your toe. It adds one more weapon to your arsenal.

In tackling you can sometimes reach the ball with your toe when you can't in any other way.

THE MAKE-UP OF THE IDEAL PLAYER

To **Tiemo Liekoski:** Head coach of the **Cleveland Force** of the **MISL.**

Question: "Could you describe the ideal player?"

Answer: "I think the player has to have a **good attitude;** he's got to have a **big heart;** he has to have a strong engine inside his chest. He must be **willing to work,** and he's got to be willing to take that **extra step** when he doesn't think he can do that. If he can do that, then I think the player can be successful. In addition to that, it's really important that the player has quickness, that he has the first step and **that he can beat the defender one on one.**"

To **Bob McNab:** Former head coach of the **Tacoma Stars** of the **MISL.**

Question: "What makes an ideal indoor player?"

Answer: "I think the consumate indoor player is a **two way player;** one who is capable of attacking skillfully, controls the ball, passes the ball well, and has good defensing skills."

"Our game at the professional level ends up coming down to one on one. We set at one v one plays, teams set at one v one plays against us. You can't cover one another like you can outdoors. You don't have the space. So basically you have to be comfortable one v one at both ends of the court."

"Throw in some character, throw in some courage, throw in some tremendous running ability. Also quickness is a great asset."

To **Roy Turner:** Head coach of the **Wichita Wings** of the **MISL.**

Question: "What would you say constitutes an ideal player in the indoor game?"

Answer: "I think there are many different types of players with strengths and weaknesses, but I think personal strength, skill, and speed and the ability to avoid injuries."

"I've always geared our team around skill, rather than work load, because to become better you can improve on peoples' work rate and endurance, but their skill level is something that takes many, many years to get to the stage whereby you can become better or worse than other teams."

One important ingredient to success in any competitive sport has nothing to do with technique or tactics.

Franz Beckenbauer calls it **fighting spirit.** You could call it the **drive** and **desire** to work at your full capacity.

All the technique and tactics in the world will get you nowhere if you only operate at ½ or ¾ potential. If you expect to win consistently, you have to **expect** to put out your full work load when necessary.

Many teams can put together a good quarter or a good half. Teams that are willing to work for themselves and each other will be more consistent. They are willing to lay it all on the line and find out how good or how bad they really are. If they get beat, so be it, but they refuse to beat themselves through lack of spirit.

Good training habits will make you physically fit. Determination to show character and pride in your rightful place, **at your own competitive level**, will help to establish your mental fitness.

Confidence is the one most important factor in performing well. Build confidence in your teammates by praise and encouragement.

Everybody makes mistakes. Don't dwell on them, and don't critize your teammates for them.

Be positive and forgiving in your attitude toward yourself and toward your fellow players. That way your game is a pleasant experience win, lose or draw. To do the best you can, and to continually improve, should be your goals.

TRAINING TIPS

Other things being equal, the correct **execution** of basic **skills** and **tactics** wins games. These skills and tactics are acquired through repetition in training until they become an ingrained part of your game.

The more advanced in skill and experience you become, the fewer the touches of the ball should be used in practice.

When a team reaches a high degree of skill, one touch play will force them to develop even further. The aim of all practice sessions should be to economize on movement in playing the ball. The more efficient your game, the more energy you have left.

Young players want to do it all on their own with a lot of solo runs or long risky passes. The best teams know when to let the ball do the work and when the player has to do it.

Consciously or sub-consciously we become what we want to become. Lots of guys are world class beer drinkers. They got that way because they wanted to, and they worked very hard at it.

Examine yourself and decide what you really want to be. If you want to become a world class ball handler, you have to work at it every chance you get. Those skills are acquired almost imperceptibly over the years in solitary practice, and small sided drills and scrimmages and pick-up games, with no pressure of winning or losing.

Some people can learn by copying moves that other people make. Some people have to work out their own. Others use a combination of both.

From the Pro's: **Stan Stemencovic**, all star forward with the **Baltimore Blast** of the **MISL** and his linemate, midfielder **Michael Collins**.

Question to Stan: "What do you think the young players should do to try to acquire the types of moves that you have?"

Answer: "I can't explain because I started to play soccer when I was five years old. I played everyday maybe four or five hours. After I was eight years old, I played six or seven hours in the street everyday. Nobody taught me. I think maybe it's just God gave me this talent."

Question: "Did you copy other players when they made a move, and try it yourself?"

Answer: "No. I tried to copy other guy's moves, but I couldn't. I just had to work with my own moves."

Michael Collins: Midfielder and linemate of Stamenkovic.

Answer: "I think what he's trying to say is that he was born with a special talent and he developed that. He realized when he was young that he had this talent and he worked on it. What he's trying to say is that **practice** is the best medicine."

Question: "Michael, what have you learned from playing with Stan?"

Answer: "When you play with Stan, you learn that he's so calm on the ball. He makes other players respect him when he has the ball."

"He has great **timing** and **balance**. His **timing** is perfect. When he scores a goal very rarely does he do it with his instep. He usually hits it with the inside of his foot. He **fakes** one way and **shoots** the other."

Question: "Michael, what have you picked up in your own game from Stan?"

Answer: "One of the things I've learned from Stan is when you're on the ball to **show the other player that you are very confident.** Also when you are near goal, I've learned a move from him to fake one way and as soon as the guy goes that way you've got the opening to take the shot. He's always told me **when you get the opportunity, shoot the ball.**"

It's been said you acquire what skill you will have by the time you are eighteen. That's setting a foolish limitation on yourself. I believe you can develop new techniques indefinitely, if you want to put in the effort that's necessary. It's your **mental attitude** that's important, **not your age.**

The ways the human body can move are infinite. You could never explore them all in eighteen years. What you lose in sheer physical drive, you make up for in finesse and smarts.

Decide what you want to be, and then **search** for the people who can teach you. Work on your own by trial and error. Read books on the subject. A lot of video tapes have come out recently on soccer skills and tactics. They would be extremely helpful. **Pele's** video, **"Pele, The Master and His Method,"** just about says it all.

In soccer, the crowds come to see the magicians in the game. You could be one of them.

Ron Newman, head coach of the San Diego Sockers, suggests you study attacking and defending at the same time.

When you are preparing an attacking strategy, consider how the defenders will react to it. The same with defensive tactics. How will the attackers react? As you work out a passing pattern, slowly go through a defensing study of how to stop the attack. The defensing study helps you to avoid poorly conceived attacks, and helps you to recognize sound attacking principles (passing to a target man, making slanting runs to shield the ball as it comes to you, avoiding dangerous square passes, etc.)

Walk through one of your attacking plays using passive defending players. You should readily see what adjustments the attacking players will have to make in order for the attack to work. Gradually have the defenders take more active roles, and see if the play still works. Keep making adjustments, perhaps with suggestions from the defending players, until the play will work at game speed. Use the same method when practicing your defending tactics. Keep changing them until you get the results you want. Studying your defensing and attacking like this will get them to work when it counts, in an actual match.

Individual skill plays an enormous part in attacking and defending. Suit your strategies to the talents of the people you're working with. In training concentrate on skills that have shown themselves to be weak. Build on techniques, tactics, and confidence at the same time.

The game boils down to two things: Being able to move the ball from one end of the court to the other; and preventing the other team from doing the same.

The first uses the following tactics:

1. The counter attack, or fast breakaway from defense.
2. Passing your way out of defense, using the goal keeper if necessary.
3. Moving the ball through the midfield with various passing combinations.
4. Creating and taking scoring chances in the attacking zone (inside the red line), using target man plays, ricochet plays off the boards, and individual dribbling and shooting abilities.

Defending against these tactics, a team has to:

1. Be alert and prepared to drop back to prevent the counter attack.
2. Learn how to use full court pressure, and how to trap the goal-keeper if the chance comes up.
3. Learn how to tightly mark man to man, so as to create tackling and intercepting opportunities.
4. Develop a combination of man to man and zone marking to clog all the passing and shooting lanes, and build the skill and tactics needed to break up passes played off the boards.

PRACTICING

Practice is important to acquire skill in any sport. Frequently local school gyms are available after school hours, and they usually make good practice courts. Avoid any gyms that have hard, sharp cornered projections in their walls. **Safety first** is the rule for any indoor practice sessions.

The skill areas that need the most attention are usually close quarter individual ball control, passing accuracy, and the use and creation of space in running off the ball.

Most gyms don't have suitable walls for withstanding hard shots on goal. They often have unprotected windows and lights. It's best to use small goals 3 or 4 feet wide and restrict any goal shots to easy push passes.

The main idea is to create a regular program of training from which you'll get the most benefit.

Don't take hard shots, because you will quickly lose your welcome if school property gets damaged.

MORE THOUGHTS ON THE GAME

If you want to be good at this game, play it every day. That's the only way to find out what works and what doesn't work for **you.** That's true of any game, or anything else you want to do. If you play it every day, and get good solid instruction from time to time from someone who understands and can play the game, the concepts of making space, timing runs, accurate passing and the rest, will come to you by doing, and copying people who can do it. The more often you play, the more you compress the learning experience into a shorter time span.

The body and mind learn by doing. So the main thing in whatever you want to become, is to do it as often as possible. Take that ninety minutes, that hour, half hour, or even fifteen minutes and do your thing. That's how you learn. Nothing takes the place of experience.

If you find this reason, or that reason, why you can't do it, then be content with a very low level of achievement, or you will be faced with continual frustration and disappointment. Do it every day for a while and you'll start to feel like a kid again, and that's what play is all about. Make no mistake about it, that hour a day is very important to you. Try it, you'll like it.

No matter what your age, once you're in reasonably good shape, daily play makes a tremendous difference. You'll be playing with mildly sore muscles from time to time, but experimentation will give you an idea of the amount of work you can stand.

Kids learn and grow with a sport, because they do it every day as a matter of course. They do it because they're kids, and they're kids because they do it. Daily practice puts your muscles in an entirely different condition than does once or twice a week activity.

When you are learning a new technique, your body and mind say, "Hold it! This is not the way we do things."

Gradually, through repetition, they grudgingly concede, "Well maybe it can be done this way." Children learn a bit quicker, because they haven't so many ingrained learning patterns to overcome, and they're more flexible.

The fundamentals of all techniques feel unnatural at first, unless you learn them at a very early age as you are growing up. Never-the-less, new techniques and skills can be learned at almost any age, but it's a two-fold process. You have to unlearn your present way, and learn the new way. It's very important that you practice daily. Foot skills come very slowly over the years, and it's easy for your body to forget if too much time elapses between training sessions.

The more skillful we become, the more our minds become free to think of tactics and our fellow players. Practice the fundamental skills of **dribbling, passing, trapping, and shooting.** (A wall is your best friend). Keep exploring new and possibly better ways to perform these skills. This adds interest to the game and it's never ending, since the combinations of our bodily movements are infinite. Watch your local first division teams when you can, as well as any professional games you can get to.

The more profound and ingrained your skills become, the easier it is to get your eyes up off the floor and to give thought to your teammates and to team tactics. There is enough to keep us interested for a lifetime. Soccer is a great habit to get into. The room for improvement is endless. It's a universal language, understood around the world, and practiced by people of all ages.

You'll never know a feeling of effortless running until you play or train five or six days a week. You won't know what real fitness is, and you won't know the fun of having your body take over the action while you lose yourself in the flow of the game.

Human beings were born for action, but you can't fool your body. It needs the daily activity in order to learn and perform with grace and ease. The only danger is you'll become addicted, and quite quickly, to daily required exercise, but that's a better addiction than most others you could get these days. As for a place to train, remember school gyms are usually there for the asking. Form a group to train and scrimmage at regular times. You could run for fifteen or twenty minutes in the morning, and play soccer for an hour at evening. Almost all of us waste more than an hour and fifteen minutes a day watching other people perform on television. It would change your life dramatically for the better. There's a big difference between watching someone do something and doing it yourself. A sample training session is given later in the book.

It's true expending energy makes you tired, but it's also true when you reach a higher level of fitness, training actually creates energy on a day to day basis. What would exhaust you if done once a week, will come easily to you if you do it every day. The body complains if you exert yourself only from time to time. It also complains if you stop doing something that you have done every day for a long time. Once you attain a good level of fitness, it's fairly easy to keep it, because the training that got you there has become a habit. Once you're over the distress of the occasional work-out, you enter the pleasurable world of daily physical performance. We find the time for a multitude of bad habits, why not resolve to form the most important good habit of daily, demanding exercise. Kids think it's fun, you will to.

The other night, between halves of a professional indoor soccer game, I watched a karate demonstration by fifty people composed of a mixture of all ages and both sexes. Their enjoyment in performing this difficult and violent sport was so obvious I had to envy them the pleasure they got from an activity that would have devastated anyone not trained in it. Their joy in their physical capability and mental composure was obvious.

You can experience the same thing. The joy of action, and the silent pleasure of mastering a difficult thing, lives inside you and changes your outlook on life.

If you dream of a future of wealth, and a retirement of ease, you're headed for trouble. Look for action every day. That's what you're meant for, and you'll never know how old you are.

One thing you notice about the really good players is their just plain honest to god running ability. They run with their knees well bent, and they take large strides, but they're always on balance. They really can run, all of the good ones. The whole game is built on running, so your running ability is a prime ingredient of your soccer ability.

The running requirements for the various age and skill levels will vary a lot, but you want to be able to match or exceed the average running ability **at your own level of play.** Fortunately, running is one of the easiest skills to develop. Everybody can run. The trick is to train in a way that benefits your sport the most.

Indoor soccer running is almost all anaerobic, high speed for short distances. To compliment this it's good to train at slow, longer distances. This helps to balance the muscles of the front and back of the legs, and builds stamina and endurance. Start easily and walk whenever you get uncomfortably tired. Try to build up to from one to two miles a day at a comfortable pace, one where you can carry on a conversation without struggling for breath. Every other day include interval sprints where you alternately sprint fifty to one hundred yards, and then walk fifty yards. Add to this backward running, side stepping, and grapevine running. On these be sure to get your heels down each step.

Start your running program slowly. If your fitness is low, start by running fifty steps and walking fifty. Gradually increase the running and decrease the walking until you can run a mile. After that it's up to you. Don't overdo the running to the point it takes available energy away from your soccer activity. The point is soccer requires running, and the best players are all great runners. Improving your running ability is the quickest and easiest way to improve your soccer ability.

Sports should help teach us to recognize what it takes to succeed. It takes time, practice, study, good instruction, conditioning, and team work.

Winning is fun, but the opportunity to play and improve is more important than winning or losing. After the game, don't look backward, don't replay your mistakes, don't second guess the referee. The fun and lesson is, just keep trying. If you make it a self improvement contest—a learning experience—then you always come out on top. People will forget your won and lost record, but the impression you leave as a person and a sportsman will linger a long time.

Work on your dribbling moves whenever you can. They are the words and phrases of your soccer language. You string them together, and with a pass you send along a message to your teammates. The more fluent your moves, the more articulate your message. Without these basic phrases and expressions, it's hard to tell what you are trying to do, and the game is reduced to a primitive physical encounter.

If the various tactics aren't broken down into their components and practiced in training sessions, the theory goes out the window the minute the action starts.

Just as in building any other skill, the tactical movements have to be practiced at walking speed and then a little faster and faster until they become a part of the team's playing style.

Introduce a little at a time so it can be **absorbed** and **understood.** Work on one or two things until they become established in the players' minds. Build your game in **small increments** and with **patience** and the results will be permanent.

COOLING DOWN

As soon as your game or training session is over, be sure to put on your sweat suit or other comfortable clothing. Avoid cooling down too fast. Take your shower **after** any cooling down process.

During competion or training the player's body and emotions are highly aroused. This arousal carries over after the activity stops. It's helpful to find some way to **safely** and **pleasantly** reduce this arousal and return the body and mind to a more relaxed state.

Stretching at this time has a most beneficial effect, mentally and physically. The muscles, joints, tendons, and ligaments are very warm and pliable, and any reclining position helps to move the blood out of the legs where it may have pooled. Stretching and abdominal breathing calm your mind and emotions quickly.

If you have any joint problems or injuries, be very careful about any stretches you might attempt. You could talk it over with your doctor or physical therapist. Execute all these movements **slowly and smoothly. Positively do not bounce into any of them.**

Stretch #1. Sit cross legged with the right leg on top. **Relax the hip joints** and allow the thighs to spread toward the floor. Raise your arms overhead and **slowly** bend forward keeping you back as flat as possible. When you've gone as far as you can with your back flat, continue the forward bend by letting your back gradually round. Let your head fall forward and relax the neck. In this position keep breathing slowly through the nose and relax the solar plexus. Keep breathing in this position for 30 to 60 seconds, more if you like. **Slowly** raise your upper body to the original sitting position. Repeat the whole procedure with the left leg crossed on top.

Stretch #1. Fig. 81

Stretch #2. Sit on your feet as shown in the illustration and **slowly** bend backward as far as you **comfortably** can go. Use your hands and forearms to slowly lower yourself. The key is to relax the ankles, knees, thighs, abdominal muscles and the soles of your feet. Continue to breathe through your nose and hold the position 10 to 30 seconds. **Slowly** rise to the starting position.

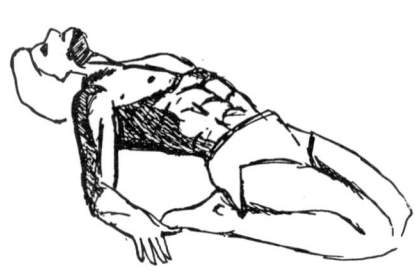

Stretch #2. Fig. 82

Stretch #3. Stay in the position in which you finished stretch #2. Sit back on your heels. Lower your upper body as far as it will go forward. Extend your arms forward with the forearms touching the floor.

Breathe slowly through the nose, making sure you completely and consciously relax everything: the soles of your feet; the ankles; the knees; the thighs; the hips; the lower back; the shoulders; the neck; the arms, wrists, and hands. Remain in this posture for up to two minutes as you tell each body part to let go and relax.

Stretch #3. Fig. 83

Stretch #4. Sit spraddle legged with your legs as far apart as is comfortable. Bend your toes back toward you, and grip them with your hands.

Straighten your legs so that the entire backs of your legs are in contact with the floor. Keep your back as flat as possible, and lean your upper body forward. When you can go no further, allow your back to round and your head to drop forward toward the floor. Breathe abdominally through the nose while you hold this position for 30 to 60 seconds. Slowly rise to sitting position. Don't pull yourself any deeper into this stretch than is comfortable.

Stretch #4. Fig. 84

Stretch #5 Kneel on your left knee, and extend your straight right leg to the side as shown. Extend your right arm and let it lie on your right leg, palm up. Raise your left arm straight overhead. Keep your head and body facing front as you bend sideways to the right. Relax your entire left side and let the weight of your upper body carry it to the right. Only stretch as far as is comfortable. Keep breathing throughout the exercise. Hold for thirty seconds and return upright. Very flexible people will be able to stretch until both arms come together. Each individual is different. **Don't** make a contest out of it. Stretch only to your **own** capacity. Repeat the stretch to the other side.

Stretch #5. Fig. 85

Stretch #6. Lie on your back, knees bent, soles of the feet flat on the floor. Put your hands behind your head, elbows flat on floor. Press both legs together toward the floor to the right. At the same time turn your head to the left and look to the left. This gives a twisting motion to the spine. It feels good, but don't strain. In time you can gradually increase this twist. Repeat left side, right side, left side, until you complete 5 repetitions each way. Hold for 2 complete breaths each time.

Stretch #6. Fig. 86

Taking a yoga class can have a remarkable effect as well. The stretches involved are all scientific, and designed to reach specific areas. Almost all present day knowledge of stretching is rooted in the ancient art of yoga. With a knowledge of yoga techniques, you can get much more from your stretching activities.

Immediately following a fight or sparring session, Jack Dempsey, the legendary heavyweight boxing champion, used to wrap himself in a sheet, lie on a table and "sweat out" until he cooled down.

There are several benefits to this. Wrapping in the sheet retains body heat, and gives it off slowly, and it absorbs perspiration. Lying down takes the weight off muscles, and combined with the retained body heat, causes a complete relaxation of body and mind. It rests the heart, and allows the blood that has pooled in the legs to recirculate freely. It diminishes the emotional arousal that accompanies strenuous physical competition. When you have cooled down to a comfortable state of body and mind, follow up with several or all of the stretches described. If you try these methods of cooling down, you'll find the feeling of well being they give is well worth the time spent. The longlasting effect of flexibility and freedom from injury will benefit you for years into the future. If you're cooling down too fast, add a blanket over the sheet.

If conditions beyond your control prevent your completing this entire cool down, experiment with all the methods, and choose the ones that seem to agree with your needs the most. If you have to neglect some of the stretches immediately following your game or work out, perhaps you can find time later that evening to complete them. Usually, moderate stretching just before bedtime will contribute to a relaxed, sleep inducing state, especially if deep abdominal breathing is used.

The Professional Game

The professional indoor game is the only active, successful professional soccer game in the country at this time.

The recent 1986 World Cup competition where Canada was involved, brought the plight of the North American professional soccer player into focus. A lot of criticism was aimed at the ability of the indoor players to adjust to and play the outdoor game at world class levels. Naturally the players needed time to adjust to the needs of the outdoor game, (which they didn't get) but without the professional indoor players, Canada would have had to play aging ex-pros or amateurs. The North American amateur game isn't played at world class levels. Right now, and for the forseeable future, the indoor game is the only professional soccer game around. Young players who don't learn the game are going to be incompletely prepared for future participation in the indoor or the outdoor game.

Players should build their game on sound tactical practices. They'll get to understand the game, and develop the abilities the pro teams are looking for.

Often players attempting to enter the professional game don't have a working knowledge of indoor principles.

They lose a lot of time and opportunities to play while they learn basic tactics. Since the indoor game is young, there is very little competent coaching available at the average indoor soccer facility. This will gradually improve, but the young player should see and study as many professional games as possible. The argument that indoor play interferes with outdoor play is unfounded. **David Norman**, who plays with the professional indoor team the **Tacoma Stars,** was considered by some the most valuable player on the 1986 Canadian World Cup team. The modern international game has become a much shorter, quick-passing game as exemplified by Argentina, France, and many other World soccer powers. That's the kind of game indoor soccer developes. Close individual and team ball control under great pressure has been the North American player's weak point. Indoor play builds this skill continously.

Regardless of what our individual attitudes toward professional sports may be, there is no question the presence of a professional league, elevates play at all levels. Without the indoor professional game, our prospects of seeing really skilled soccer players in action would be very bleak at this time. The professional game is the catalyst that inspires improvement and advancement of skills and tactics at all levels of the sport. The indoor game could eventually affect the make-up of the outdoor game and perhaps make it a more exciting spectator sport.

A Sample Practice Session
Warm-Up

    A. Plies

        1. One set of plies in Pos. #1.
        2. One set of plies in Pos. #2 (right foot in front)
        3. One set of plies in Pos.#2 (left foot in front)
        These three sets make a series. Repeat the series three times.

                                                                            Elapsed time 5 min.

    B. Stretches

        Do stretches #1 through #6. (lightly)

                                                                             Elapsed time 8 to 10 min.

    C. Dribbling, passing, and juggling moves.

        (the players make up their own)

                                                                               Elapsed time 5 min.

After you are warmed-up:

    D. Do any two passing drills.

                                                                            Elapsed time 10 min.

    E. Work on two combination plays or set plays.

                                                                            Elapsed time 15 min.

    F. Work on two passing off the boards plays.

                                                                            Elapsed time 15 min.

    G. Scrimmage.

                                                                            Elapsed time 30 min.

Cool Down:

        Do Stretches #1 through #6.

                                                                            Elapsed time 10 min.

The total time of the work out is approximately 90 minutes. It's good to outline each training session beforehand, so that you cover all the material over a period of time. Scrimmaging is fun and very useful, but don't forget to practice the other things as well. Try to make the entire session as game-related as possible so that you have fun and learn new things at the same time.

Note: Regardless of how you outline your training session, allot an absolute minimum of fifteen minutes for the warm-up, more if possible. Do nothing strenuous until you are completely warm and have induced a good sweat. Wearing a sweat suit hastens the body's warm-up.

Go For It.

ESTABLISHING SET PATTERNS OF PLAY.

Less experienced amateur teams should make a real effort to standardize some of their ball movement patterns. Very often they find themselves almost unable to play, simply because there is no consensus among the players about what formations to use, and about what runs and passes to make.

Each team should work out several basic patterns of play, that will let them move the ball about in a sensible manner on various parts of the court.

First: Develop a scheme that will get you out of your own defensive zone quickly and safely. The 2-1-2 formation will work well here. See Fig. 78.

Second: Once the ball is worked into the opponents' half, work on several ways to create a shot on goal. There are many such attacking plays shown here in the book.

Even if you are up against superior skill, sound tactical movement will give you a chance at winning.

When you get the ball, you know where to look for your teammates. They will take up familiar positions, they'll make familiar runs, and they'll make familiar passes. This means you can play the ball quicker and with more confidence. It makes the team feel they know what they are doing, and that's a big step in the right direction. You build your game around set patterns of play, and then vary it to suit requirements.

Your team should work out set ways that will get them out of the defensive end and then create scoring opportunities. When you have established these several set ways to move the ball, and can execute them with confidence, you can gradually add additional movements to give a little variety to your game. If you find something that works, keep doing it until it doesn't work anymore.

In the beginning, establish standard patterns with which everyone can become familiar. That gives your team structure, coherence, and **confidence**.

SPECIAL CONDITION SCRIMMAGES

Special condition scrimmages can develope and sharpen specific areas of play.

Play a scrimmage using each of the following special conditons.
1. All goals must be scored directly from a one-two pass. After receiving the return pass, the scorer is allowed no more than two touches before shooting.
2. All goals must be scored directly from a rebound off the boards. The shooter is allowed no more than two touches to score.
3. The shooter must beat at least one player with a dribble before shooting on goal.
4. All play is limitied to three, two, or one touch.

If any of the above conditions are violated, ball possession passes to the other team and play resumes with a free kick. Decide what particular areas of your game need emphasis, and work on them through special condition scrimmages.